How on Earth Do We Live Now?

Natural Capital,

Deep Ecology,

and the Commons

Quaker Institute for the Future Pamphlet Series

1— *Fueling our Future: A Dialogue about Technology, Ethics, Public Policy, and Remedial Action* by Ed Dreby and Keith Helmuth, Coordinators with Judy Lumb, Editor, 2009

2— *How on Earth Do We Live Now? Natural Capital, Deep Ecology, and the Commons* by David Ciscel, Barbara Day, Keith Helmuth, Sandra Lewis, and Judy Lumb, 2011

3— *Genetically Modified Crops: Promises, Perils, and the Need for Public Policy* by Anne Mitchell, with Pinayur Rajagopal, Keith Helmuth, and Susan Holtz, 2011

Forthcoming:
4— *How Does Social Transformation Happen? A Guide to Values Development* by Leonard Joy

Quaker Institute for the Future Pamphlets aim to provide critical information and understanding born of careful discernment on social, economic, and ecological realities, inspired by the testimonies and values of the Religious Society of Friends (Quakers). We live in a time when social and ecological issues are converging toward catastrophic breakdown. Human adaptation to social, economic and planetary realities must be re-thought and re-designed. **Quaker Institute for the Future Pamphlets** are dedicated to this calling based on a spiritual and ethical commitment to "right relationship" with Earth's whole commonwealth of life.

Quaker Institute for the Future
<quakerinstitute.org>

How on Earth Do We Live Now? Natural Capital, Deep Ecology, and the Commons

David Ciscel, Barbara Day, Keith Helmuth, Sandra Lewis, and Judy Lumb

A Circle of Discernment Report from Quaker Institute for the Future

June 2011

—Quaker Institute for the Future Pamphlet 2—

Published for Quaker Institute for the Future by *Producciones de la Hamaca*, Caye Caulker, Belize <producciones-hamaca.com>

ISBN: 978-976-8142-28-3

How on Earth Do We Live Now? Natural Capital, Deep Ecology, and the Commons is the second in a series of Quaker Institute for the Future Pamphlets: Series ISBN: 978-976-8142-21-4

Producciones de la Hamaca is dedicated to:

—Celebration and documentation of Earth
   and all her inhabitants,
—Restoration and conservation of Earth's
   natural resources,
—Creative expression of the sacredness of
   Earth and Spirit.

Contents

Preface

A radical re-assessment is underway on what it will take to prevent our industrial-commercial civilization from sliding sideways into the ditch of increasing ecological breakdown and repeated economic collapse. On one hand, the environmental movement, that put its faith in regulation, is being written off by some of its veterans as a failure. On the other, the complete inability of banking, investment, and business to prevent the recent catastrophic financial breakdown highlights failures of our current economic system. If capitalism and environmentalism are both failing, where do we turn to understand the fate of the human-Earth relationship?

Many folks are now trying to engage the social and economic crisis from an ecological footing. We draw a sense of well-being and sanity from the beauty and evident wisdom of Earth's ecosystems and their capacity to support life. Yet we see the web of life disrespected, degraded and disrupted on every hand by economic activity. We see more and more clearly that the frontlines of critical change—the hinge points of ecological restoration and social equity—are log-jammed in an economy that is both dysfunctional and out of control. As David Ciscel put it in a 2007 article in *Quaker Eco-Bulletin* (*QEB*) *"It's the economy, Friends."*[1]

Ciscel's article introduced the consideration of air, land, water, minerals, plants, animals, and services provided by ecosystems as "natural capital." In a follow-up 2009 article Ciscel suggested that bringing natural capital under the management of the mainstream economic system will result in full-cost accounting of the human impact on the environment and is essential to reversing our current destructive trends.[2]

Prompted by Ciscel's articles, the QEB editorial team felt it was important to explore the large question emerging from the field of ecological economics: Is Earth a subset of the human economy or is the human economy a subset of the biosphere? The predominant, technological, human-centered approach assumes that Earth is a subset of the global economy that functions primarily to benefit humans. Drawing on both science and ancient indigenous wisdom, the approach of deep ecology

8

assumes that humans are one species among many in the larger community of life on Earth, and we cannot thrive economically, or otherwise, unless the whole web of life thrives.

The natural capital and deep ecology approaches both address the question: "How on Earth do we live now?" Both approaches operate within the understanding that the high energy industrial economy is crashing into the reality of Earth's ecology, and that a massive environmental crisis is unfolding from this incoherent human-Earth relationship. Within the movement for "Earth restored,"[3] the natural capital approach and the deep ecology approach are often in tension and sometimes in conflict. Natural capital people can become impatient with what seems like an impractical spiritualizing of the human-Earth relationship. Deep ecology people can become alarmed at the idea that what really counts in saving the natural environment is to get an appropriate monetary value assigned to every resource.

Realizing that we wanted to explore these two world views in some depth, we asked David Ciscel to join the *QEB* editorial team in a Circle of Discernment process under the auspices of the Quaker Institute for the Future (QIF). The Institute helps create small study groups that collaboratively research and discuss a particular topic or concern with the goal of producing a pamphlet-length text that informs readers about the concern and helps equip them for witness and action.

We undertook this collaborative discernment in the hope of bringing to light understanding that was beyond our individual abilities. For two years we worked individually in Canada, the U.S., and Belize. We conferred by conference call in the manner of Friends, sometimes speaking out of the international silence and sometimes in guided discussion. Each of these bimonthly calls has led us to a new and surprising point of "knowing" that could not have been reached by discussion and debate of a conventional sort. Our goal was to engage in this unique process of group learning about subjects of deep interest to each of us. We are pleased to share the results of our inquiry with others who are attempting to forge new pathways to ecologically sound and socially equitable living.

We lifted up the natural capital approach on the one hand, and the deep ecology approach on the other. We hoped that by working out their similarities, contrasts, and conflicts, we might arrive at their mutually beneficial contributions to an emerging world view. We see this dialogue as vital for accessing the deep structures of human consciousness and for bringing significant change to institutional and on-the-street economic behavior.

We found that the two converged in the reality of Earth's commons and the common good for all species that inhabit Earth. We explored the history and development of current public policies in regard to two essential parts of Earth's commons: property and water. We believe that both require major changes in governance. We studied systems of governance from private property to self-governing, community-based, trust organizations and the nature of human behavior from individualistic to cooperative. We asked what unique contributions Friends bring to the table as we all face the realization of the enormity of the change that is needed for a sustainable and just human-Earth relationship.

While in this pamphlet we speak as members of the Religious Society of Friends (Quakers), we realize that many other people connected to many other groups are working on the same issues that concerns us, and that it is only as we all work together that such light as we have may be kindled into effective action.

We came to feel a deep purpose in this dialogue and are grateful for ongoing conversations with a number of QIF associates and reviewers. In particular we thank Charlie Blanchard, Ed Dreby, Tom Head, Patricia McBee, Ed Snyder, and Shelley Tanenbaum for reviewing the manuscript and offering helpful comments. We have appreciated the support of the QIF Board of Trustees (*p. 91*).

We hope that our work will be helpful for Friends and the wider community of seekers who are determined to bring the human-Earth relationship into a sustainable balance and that it will spur the readers to take up their own study that will lead to action. In this way, our work can unfold to good effect beyond the limitations of our modest efforts.

David Ciscel, Barbara Day, Keith Helmuth,
Sandra Lewis, and Judy Lumb

Chapter 1
How on Earth Do We Live Now?

Man in his misguidance has powerfully interfered with Nature. He has devastated the forests, and thereby even changed the atmospheric conditions and the climate. Some species of plants and animals have become entirely extinct through man, although they were essential in the economy of Nature. Everywhere the purity of the air is affected by smoke and the like, and the rivers are defiled. These and other things are serious encroachments upon Nature, which men nowadays entirely overlook but which are of the greatest importance, and at once show their evil effect not only on the plants but upon animals as well.
—Johann Wolfgang von Goethe (1832)[4]

How on Earth do we live now? This question is haunting the human prospect, as well as the future of many other species. We are wavering on the edge of an almost impossible thought: The way of life we have been conditioned to regard as "normal" is destroying the life support capacity of the planet.

In the eighteenth Century, slavery was regarded as a "normal" part of economic life in the British Empire. In 1791 a report was made to a Select Committee on the Abolition of the Slave Trade of the British House of Commons that stated:

A trade which disgraces the national character, which is productive of unexampled misery to the human race and must sooner or later bring down the vengeance of God on the nation that pursues it, must be impolitic indeed, if it has not the plea of necessity for its continuance.[5]

11

The industrial-commercial way of life, as it moves ever deeper into the tissues of Earth's ecological arrangements, is in precisely these circumstances. We may not see the ecological crisis as the vengeance of God, but the scale of biodiversity loss now in play, and the consequences that can be clearly foreseen, have launched something truly uncanny into our consciousness.

We know it is a human-induced crisis, but the political, legal, and economic institutions responsible for the destruction of Earth's ecology are highly resistant to changing their behavior and stopping the destruction. Just as the wealth accumulation of 18th Century Anglo-American capitalism was tied to slavery and the slave trade, there is now a tacit agreement between political, industrial, business, and financial leaders on one side, and consumers/citizens on the other, that in order to maintain and advance the industrial-commercial way of life, it is acceptable to progressively degrade the functional integrity of the biosphere. It is not an exaggeration to say, "But this is absurd!" And this sense of absurdity, this sense that something is fundamentally wrong with our mode of adaptation, is a powerful boost for course correction toward Earth restored.

Shortening the Future

We have been hearing a lot recently about the consumer economy "going over a cliff." Even *New York Times* columnist Thomas Friedman, once an unabashed booster of full-tilt globalization, has become aware of the need for ecological management and has abandoned belief in the viability of an economy based on endless growth. It may be tempting to think it would be just as well for this unsustainable economy to go over the cliff, except that it will take a huge swath of Earth's ecological and social integrity with it. The chaos, disruption, and violence likely to come with the continuing breakdown of Earth's ecological and economic systems is staggering to contemplate.

Although much of human history, especially modern history, is the story of change, most folks feel the way we live now is the way it should be, and they pretty much expect it can, should, and will go on forever. "Isn't this normal?" But today's world is neither inevitable nor sustainable.

For long stretches of time, in many regions of Earth, human groups achieved highly successful adaptations to their bioregions, resulting in the sense that their way of life was the right way. They could easily envision their life ways carrying on indefinitely. For example, traditional Iroquois cultural guidance gauges present actions by their effect on the next seven generations.[6]

Wherever industrial civilization has taken hold, it has overlaid this ancient sense of continuity with a sense of change. With the widespread use of fossil fuels, the rate of change and progress dramatically increased. Our definition of a "normal" way of life came to include ever more goods and services, better living standards, and constantly improving health care. International trade and economic globalization became the conduit for advancing the consumer economy.

Almost everyone in modern Western nations has grown up to expect this high energy industrial way of life will go on forever, constantly achieving greater heights of convenience, luxury, and wealth. At least those lucky enough to catch the wave and learn the art of surfing change and opportunity have come to see the world this way. Domestically and globally many have been marginalized in this pursuit of more and more, and caught in the undertow of progress. They either drown or end up in the backwaters of poverty, now thought of as "collateral damage."

But now the great sense of optimism about the future of industrial-commercial civilization is fading. The ideology of progress cannot be mentioned now without irony. As ecological economist Herman Daly points out, economic growth in the advanced industrial world is chalking up more liabilities than benefits and has become "uneconomic." Yet, the drive for economic growth goes on. The answer to every problem of the economy is more economic growth. Any slowdown in growth threatens a slide into recession. Recession threatens a crash into depression. Depression threatens the massive disruption of business activity, investment, and employment income, and access to the means of life. This structural failure of the consumer economy is prevented only by endless economic growth, even at the cost of increasing environmental destruction. This is not progress; it is a trap. It is well past time to ask our economists and our policy makers why our economy must continue to grow in order to avoid crashing. What do they think will happen if we go over the cliff of Earth's ecological capacity? Do they have a plan for some new human adaptation that does not depend on the integrity of Earth's ecosystems, some new technology that will come to our rescue and sustain our economy?

A shrinking number of experts with a shrinking aura of credibility are telling us that we can depend on technological innovation to come up with whatever is needed to keep this show on the road. They cannot envision any alternative to unlimited economic growth. But now this faith is becoming increasingly unbelievable. Now is the time to think hard about the distinction between what the earth sciences tell us about our biospheric situation and the fantasy that humans are somehow exempt from the processes that govern Earth's ecosystems.[7]

Ecological economists are calculating the question of whether our economic vehicle is yet approaching a point of detour, or if it has already overshot the cliff's edge, and, like the cartoon character, Wile E. Coyote, is now running full tilt in the open air over the abyss? There is discouraging evidence that this is probably the case.

The speed with which systemic financial fraud, economic volatility, disintegration of social trust, loss of biodiversity, biotic uptake of environmental toxins, and diminution of Earth's life support capacity are now piling onto each other, suggests we are already deep into an overshoot position. If this is the case, the question is: Will our economic situation suffer the fate of Wile E. Coyote when at last he looks down, sees his situation, and then precipitously crashes? The breakdown of the financial system in 2008 was an example of this reaction.

Wile E. Coyote, of course, is never really injured. Even if a big chunk of the cliff's edge breaks loose and flattens him into the dirt, he crawls out and lives to strut his stuff another day. This, too, is part of the archetypal economic fantasy that is endemic to market fundamentalism. The market goes up, the market goes down, but it *always* bounces back. This faith, however, is now confronted with the reality that ecosystems can fail; they can be disturbed to the point that biotic degeneration can make them progressively less habitable for an increasing number of species, including the human. The market goes up, the market goes down, the market goes back up—until it doesn't. Then what?

Getting a Grip and Changing Course

Global geologic forces in the past have resulted in Earth uninhabitable by humans,[8] but now human economic activity has become a geologic force, a force capable of changing Earth systems.[9] This fact has not fully penetrated the minds of politicians and policy-makers. If this reality continues to be ignored, a catastrophic crash seems inevitable. If realization dawns soon enough, a glide path to a safe landing may still be possible, though probably through some very rough weather.

The question, "**how** on Earth do we live now?" is an exclamation of distress as we wake up to the realization that what we thought of as normal progress has brought us to this crisis. Even the most sober-minded earth-system scientists are alarmed at the accelerating pace of the crisis which is potentially catastrophic for the planet's biodiversity and suicidal for the human species. But this question can also be asked as "how on Earth **do** we live now?" What makes sense? What is practical? What policy and institutional changes do we need? How do we get started with a new kind of adaptation? What specific changes will set up a course correction? How we humans organize our economy is key to answering these questions. The longer we continue our ecologically destructive economic behavior, the harder it will be to retain or restore habitats that support life. The next two chapters describe two different approaches to answer these questions: the natural capital approach and the deep ecology approach.

15

Chapter 2
The Natural Capital Approach

Capitalism, as practiced, is a financially profitable, unsustainable aberration in human development. It neglects to assign any value to the largest of the capital stocks it employs—the natural resources and living systems, as well as the social and cultural systems that are the basis of human capital.

—Paul Hawken, Amory Lovins, and I. Hunter Lovins[10]

For the past three centuries, humans have experimented with new ways to organize their economic activity. The changes have been structural and technological but, most fundamentally, they are energy-based. When we took more coal out of the mines, it was based on steam-powered pumps that kept the mines free of water. When we developed machine-made fabric and clothing, it was mechanical machines powered by water or coal-fired steam that made it possible. Fossil-fuel-based industrial economies have been dirty, chaotic, and dramatically inequitable. In addition, wars have been fought over how the industrial economy should be organized or who should control it. Two things happened over the past century: (1) the market economy won the battle of how to organize the economy, and (2) corporate elites have controlled much of its operation.

In many ways the market-based economy has been a huge success. It has produced and distributed goods and services to more people, to wider areas of the globe, and at a faster rate than could have been imagined less than a century ago. The results are not particularly equitable, but the quantities are large and the qualities of goods are very high. The industrial economy has left almost no portion of the globe untouched. People all over the world have felt the pull of the economy to raise their standard of living.

But it is the same economy that is now failing the whole Earth. And it is failing for a simple reason. The industrial economy has filled up the natural world without so much as a "thank you." In its early years, the bad effects of the industrial economy were limited and localized. Steel production may have polluted a particular river valley, or an oil refinery or paper mill may have killed all the fish in a local stream or lake, but those were seen as economic externalities that could be mitigated. The industrial economy hardly noticed how much it needed that natural world to make all the goods that producers and consumers demanded. Even where natural resources were priced, e.g. iron ore, coal and petroleum, the revenue from the sale did not go to develop alternatives to non-renewable resources and clean up waste, or, in the case of renewable resources, like wood fiber and fish, did not go to ensure replenishment.

In economic terms, we are using up our natural capital. As the economy grows and grows, it acts in an imperial manner. What used to belong to other species turns into property of humans; what used to be open landscape becomes new subdivisions; and what used to be considered "useless" land, is transformed into useable farmland. But modern industrial economies have largely operated on the assumption that these portions of Earth were just free. And, sadly, they were. There were no natural courts enforcing payment for use of air, land or water.

Our current industrial system is a major obstacle to the goal of Earth restored. The economic system has filled up the world, displacing everything else—the nature that feeds our souls and the natural systems that sustain our lives. Most of us in the industrialized world see our lives as totally dependent on current modes of production and consumption, and many in developing countries are seeking to emulate our affluence. What can we do given this reality?

From the perspective of natural capitalism, the time when the natural world can occur naturally is gone. Earth often regenerates when we step out of the way, but there is no indication that we, humans as a group, have any inclination to do that. So the end result of seeking Earth restored is most likely Earth managed to minimize the impact of economic activity. If we start from where we are, the outcomes will, by the processes employed, result in sub-optimal outcomes. That is, Earth restored will not be natural Earth, but it could be Earth where many species of life survive and prosper. Just as our daily bread comes from the bread factory, not our kitchens; so our water, our forests, our wild habitats, and our clean air will come from the green factory, not because it just exists—like it did sometime in the distant past.

This perspective suggests that we need to start from where we are, not where we wish to be or where a better world would have been. An essential first step is to introduce into our existing economic models the idea of natural capital and to create economic incentives to use our natural capital sustainably.

Building Natural Capital

Industrial capital is a normal feature of capitalist economies. It is made up of the machines, buildings, and financial investments that make capitalism work. In today's world, capital is owned and controlled by the giant corporations that dominate the economic landscape. Capital has several properties: (1) it has laws and accounting rules to help it be self-renewing (depreciation funds), (2) it earns a profit (interest) for its services, and (3) it is perpetual (maintains value) if well-managed.

Capital is usually backed by securities—stocks and bonds that are expected to grow in value over time and to pay dividends to their owners. Most of us also think of education and training as human capital—an investment that pays off during the rest of our lives in better jobs and higher incomes.

Natural capital is the environmental equivalent of industrial and human capital. The natural capital approach gives ecosystems and their natural resources value within the economy. In a world full of economy, we need to change our approach to the use of natural ecosystems, that is, we need to create a system of natural capital. Once we restructure our legal system so that ecosystems are given the characteristics of property, corporate owners will respect natural capital within the public domain. Right now, we allow property owners to receive income without paying fees to the rest of society for their use of the environment. With natural capital, society has the right to demand payment for ecosystem services or depreciation.

It is important to note that, at the moment, there really is no such thing as natural capital. There are important eco-subsystems. Forests help regulate the amounts of greenhouse gases, hold the soil in place, and are sources of life for other plants and animals. Wind, rainfall, cloud formations and other climatic processes help regulate the climate. The water-waste-recycling system is made up of water vapor, soil, and plants. These services, provided by natural ecosystems, are so many that listing them would take pages. And these ecosystem services are only the beginning. In addition, there are mineral, plant and animal resources that exist within or as part of the natural ecosystems.

Calling these things "natural capital" is important in order to make them visible in the economy. Natural capital is a way to make all the natural ecosystems part of the buying and selling that is integral to the modern industrial economy. The economy, with its very focused material worldliness, is already far too dominant a component of Earth that we live on. To turn the rest of Earth into natural capital may seem like just the wrong step. But as long as the natural world is outside our economic system, it will continue to be free and that will continue its destruction. Creating natural capital within our current economic system could be a first step toward overhauling the entire economic system into one that is sustainable on a finite Earth.

As the major corporations of the economic world slowly come to recognize the necessity of rehabilitating the natural world, a strong commitment to social justice will be needed even more. Building an economy that pays for the maintenance of natural capital means that income must be redistributed to pay for ecosystem services. The system must be constructed so that this income redistribution does not take from the poor, powerless, and marginalized people of the world, but rather enriches and empowers them.

Changing the Economy

The modern economy is highly organized over large geographic distances. To produce, distribute and consume, we use planning, administrative rules and market transactions. Property, whether social (public) or corporate (private) in origin, is at the heart of the economic enterprise. And property always earns a financial return, one which is payment based, either on its productivity from production and consumption, or on its scarcity.

If users of air, water and resources had to pay for the sustainability of their use, then many activities would cease altogether while others would become vastly more expensive as the true costs become incorporated in the selling price of various products. Examples are systems that have been put forward as alternative solutions to global climate change—the carbon tax or the cap-and-trade approach. The carbon tax is applied to the use of coal, oil and gas, thus limiting the input of more greenhouse gases into the climate system. The cap-and-trade system establishes a cap on the amount of carbon emitted and a market for transactions in carbon allowances. Both systems are based on using the economy to address the climate crisis.

To work, the natural capital method requires rules, institutions, and regulatory structures, but most importantly, prices. Prices are inflated to restrict polluting forms of production and consumption. Greener forms of consumption are encouraged by restructuring the incentives of the market system. The prices make it too expensive to use resources unsustainably. This results in a regulated market Earth, a market-managed system of ecosystems.

Beginning to think in terms of natural capital builds a process for ecological stability by accepting the fact that Earth is full. The economy, with natural capital included, becomes the whole Earth. Ecosystems, animals, and resources all are a subset of buying and selling. But they would be inside—valued, protected by property contracts, and preserved for the future benefit of the economy. If we build an economic system that creates natural capital out of Earth's ecosystems, we can set in motion a set of processes that are improvements over today's world.

Chapter 3
The Deep Ecology Approach

In the beginning, we were told that the human beings who walk about on Earth have been provided with all the things necessary for life. We were instructed ... to show great respect for all the beings on this Earth. We are shown that our... well-being depends on the well-being of the Vegetable Life, that we are close relatives of the four-legged beings. ... We give a greeting and thanksgiving to the many supporters of our own lives—the corn, squash, beans, wind, rain, and sun. ... We walk about with great respect, for Earth is a very sacred place.

—The Hau de no sau nee[11]

A deep ecology perspective calls us to look to nature for guidance in creating new social, and economic arrangements.[12] For example, how can we draw on our knowledge of how ecosystems thrive and change in nature to help us design resilient and sustainable economic and social systems? To what extent do our human economic and social arrangements acknowledge the reality that we are all connected and dependent on each other and on the larger web of life for our health and well-being? What can we learn about optimizing the flows of human energy and its products from the dynamics of the flows of energy and matter on the planet, the shifting balance between entropy and the creation of order? In seeking technological solutions to human challenges, can we tap the vast store of research and development already done by nature through the evolutionary process to mimic solutions found in nature to solve similar problems?

Industrial capitalism was designed and developed largely without regard to such questions, and we are now dealing with the consequences of this failure. Natural capitalism seeks to moderate and even reverse this destruction by using familiar tools from industrial capitalism, but natural capitalism leaves the basic assumptions of industrial capitalism mostly unchanged. It attempts to solve our ecological crises with the same mindset and tools that created them. The urgency of our situation calls us to question these old assumptions and devise new ways to conduct human affairs based on a different understanding of the human-Earth relationship.

Without the gifts of nature that sustain us—sun, water, air, soil, plants, animals, and Earth cycles, and the processes that keep them going—there would be no life, no goods, no human economy. To relate to these gifts of nature as commodities, the primary function of which is to create wealth for humans, is a fundamental flaw of modern, industrial capitalism.

Understanding and Protecting

In contrast, a deep ecology perspective calls us to remember with reverence and gratitude that nature's gifts, functioning as a whole, make life on Earth possible for us and all other species. From this perspective we have no right to create wealth for ourselves from these gifts if, in so doing, we make access to them impossible for other humans or other species. Rather we have a responsibility to care for these gifts and to help ensure their continued availability and vitality for future generations.

How can we care for Earth's gifts? First and foremost we must protect the health and vitality of these gifts. The California Academy of Sciences in San Francisco's Golden Gate Park recognizes this in its stated mission "to explore, explain and protect the natural world."[13] This venerable, science-based institution has chosen to go beyond exploring and explaining the natural world—the traditional realms of science—to take a strong public advocacy position to protect life on Earth.

The Academy's culture and operations also mirror its commitment to sustainable use of Earth's resources—energy, water, waste management, transportation, purchasing and food. Its public education programs highlight the living world and its connection to the changing global environment. Academy research focuses on the origins and maintenance of life's diversity, and its expeditions roam the world, gathering scientific data to answer two questions, "How has life evolved?" and "How can it be sustained?"

What if the entire scientific enterprise of our country and our world functioned within the framework of a commitment to explore, explain and protect the natural world? What if economics, politics, business, religion, medicine, agriculture, and education functioned as if protecting Earth's resources was an integral part of their missions?

While one can say that the purpose of economic science is to explore and explain the dynamics of human economic activity, few economists would suggest that part of their professional mandate is to protect the health of the natural world. What if the same amount of human intelligence and creativity that is now directed toward maximizing economic growth and efficiency was applied to creating human economic systems that enhance and protect Earth's ability to sustain life now and in the future?

Management or Adaptation?

From the perspective of deep ecology, nature is the ultimate source of the human economic enterprise and protecting the health and vitality of our natural wealth should be fundamental to the theory and practice of economics. Natural capitalism's idea of "managing Earth" implies a world view that sees humans as dominant and separate from nature. It is an expression of human hubris. Deep ecologists believe that humans will never "manage" Earth, because ultimately the forces of nature are much more powerful than we are.

We can, of course, cause great havoc on Earth systems, as we are now on the climate, but we cannot "manage" the climate system. Human impact on the climate system or the water system or any other system has consequences, predictable or unforeseen, which we cannot escape. Nature bats last. We can, however, manage ourselves as individuals and we can work to manage the collective actions of our species to minimize our impact on Earth's life support systems. Some of the theories and tools of traditional economics can help us in this project.

This is a tall order given the size of the human population, the inadequacies of current economic models for tracking and valuing human economic activities and natural resources, and a mindset that has, for too long, viewed Earth primarily as a warehouse of commodities for humans to use for their exclusive benefit. Thinking of Earth as a "green factory" that is the source of our water, our forests, our wild habitats, and our clean air is an example of this mindset. This mindset believes these gifts of nature should be managed by the human economic system rather than function according to natural systems of which they are a part. But as the ecological economist Herman Daly[14] has pointed out, the economy is a subsystem of Earth's system, not the other way around:

The most important change in recent times has been the enormous growth of one subsystem of Earth, namely the economy, relative to the total system, the ecosphere. ... The closer the economy approaches the scale of the whole Earth, the more it will have to conform to the physical behavior mode of Earth. That behavior mode is a steady state—a system that permits qualitative development but not aggregate quantitative growth.[15]

The physical, chemical and biological systems that govern Earth are basic because they underlie all other wealth. Economists, politicians, business owners, and the rest of us need to have a deep understanding of how these systems function and learn how to conduct our economic activities in ways that do not undermine or disrupt these processes. This is very different from the natural capitalism idea of bringing these natural systems more and more under the management of the economic system, or making them follow the rules of market-based capital. The 2008 financial crisis showed us the fallacies and unreality of the rules governing capital—trillions of dollars evaporated into the ether in a matter of months. How can we entrust all that is essential for life on Earth solely to the workings of such a flawed human system?

Realizing Potential

Our ancestors, ourselves, and our children have all been given the most amazing gift of life because our home planet embodies the conditions that bring forth and support life. So far as we know now, it is the only planet fit for humans and other earthly life. A planetarium show at the California Academy of Science, "Fragile Planet," takes us on a voyage that begins from the Academy's living roof, lifts up through the atmosphere to gain an astronaut's view of Earth, then travels to the Moon, Mars, and beyond to search for other planets that might host life. It returns to Earth having identified some possible candidates in far flung places in the universe but found nothing definitive. On touchdown the voice-over narrative ends with a brief phrase that describes the human species and the responsibility that goes with the amazing gift we have been given: "Bright child of the planet, protector of Life."

We humans are bright and clever, and capable of brilliance in meeting our needs, in following our dreams and curiosity, and then reflecting on what we have done. The fact that we can explore and explain much about life on Earth is essential if we are to go beyond exploring and explaining to actually protecting life. Will we remain immature, irresponsible beings refusing to accept the responsibility that goes along with our unique gifts? Will we abandon our single-minded pursuit of human well-being without regard to the cost to the whole community of life? If we are to grow into maturity as a species, we must choose to bend the arc of our knowledge and brilliance—whether in science, economics, technology, commerce, or any other realm of the human enterprise—toward protecting life and ensuring that future generations of all species can enjoy the same gift of life we have been given. This choice cannot be an afterthought, but the foundation and the framework that shapes the whole human-Earth relationship.

We now face two enormous challenges: (1) stopping the impacts of the human economic enterprise that are destroying Earth's life support systems, and (2) creating new social, political, and economic institutions that support rather than undermine the capacity of Earth to provide these essential gifts of life.

These challenges pose difficult choices about how to proceed, but clearly the choices we make will reflect assumptions about how things are or should be on this planet, assumptions about the right place of humans within planetary life. Are we humans stewards? kin? masters? co-evolutionists? Our choices will reflect how we perceive human nature. Are we humans self-interested? empathic? independent? interdependent? cooperative? competitive? rational? irrational? How capable are humans of expanding our circle of active caring and concern to encompass ever-widening spheres of relationship? What are the values and ethics that should guide human behavior, particularly economic behavior? An ecological world view requires radically rethinking our assumptions and making changes that reflect a mature understanding of our place in the commonwealth of life on Earth.

Chapter 4
Shaping a New Order

Having been a student of economics and a business person most of my life, I can easily argue in the morning that protecting Earth's ecosystems can best be achieved by an appropriate monetary valuation of "natural capital" and full-cost accounting. But in the evening, as I gaze at the globe in my library, and feel Earth and its encompassing life rolling along through eons of cosmic experience, the confidence of my morning calculations are swept into doubt.

—Keith Helmuth[16]

Which strategy will work and work quickly enough to turn around the current downward trends in Earth's viability? In the current social and political environment, the distinctions between natural capitalism and deep ecology seem to fade in the light of overwhelming opposition to any systemic changes. But if the costs of climate change increase dramatically in temperate regions of Earth—crop failures, large population die-offs, or water shortages—the need for change will become more urgent. The two approaches, natural capital and deep ecology, could be complementary rather than conflicting in addressing that urgency. In any case, systemic change requires much greater awareness that humans are only one among many species and our survival is dependent upon the survival of the whole commonwealth of life.

If we keep trying to fine tune the industrial-commercial system in ways that reduce the rate of ecosystem destruction, we run the risk of collapse of ecological resilience. High technology, the universal commodification of resources, and global financial management will fail when Earth's ecosystems are no longer capable of renewal.

If we rapidly back off our intensive energy use and high material consumption to allow Earth's ecosystems to begin to restore resilience and biodiversity, we run the risk of collapsing global monetary systems and bringing on an era of human adaptation that is significantly less convenient and strikingly more labor intensive than how we live now.

We are faced with a choice of risks—risking the collapse of the ecological basis of Earth's biodiversity or risking the collapse of the industrial-commercial way of life. The natural capital approach tends to run the first risk. The deep ecology approach tends to run the second. Both are part of a profound re-evaluation of the human-Earth relationship.

No matter how attractive full-cost accounting and right-pricing, the natural capital approach cannot credibly fall back on the market economy's notion of the "invisible hand." No matter how attractive the ecologically sound design of human settlement and resource use, the deep ecology approach cannot credibly fall back on the notion of "natural harmony" in a subsistence economy.

Adaptation is a characteristic of life in all circumstances and management is a feature of adaptation. Natural capital and deep ecology, while harboring different concepts of management and projecting different practices of adaptation, must deal with the same interlocking ecological, economic and social crisis. The hard work of adaptation in the conditions of contemporary existence hands its work orders to both schools of thought.

The natural capital approach manages to make the human domination of Earth's ecosystems the least damaging possible. The deep ecology approach manages to make Earth's ecosystems and biodiversity as resilient as possible. Both manage human impact: the first, to continue human wealth accumulation and high-level convenience, the latter to continue ecosystem integrity and high-level biodiversity. The first is willing to take the risk of adapting Earth process to human

29

settlement and wealth accumulation. The latter is willing to risk adapting human settlements and wealth restriction to Earth process. Each approach reflects a particular ethos—for natural capitalism it is one of mastery or exploitation and for deep ecology one of interdependence and precaution. In more conventional terms, it is the difference between the developer and the conservationist.

Making the Road by Walking

Not only does this tension emerge between persons in their differing approaches to understanding and action, but it can also emerge within persons as they play different roles in different circumstances. Understanding and action may change as circumstances change. Clearly this is not an either/or situation. A farmer who is devoted to ecologically sound agriculture may actually increase the fertility of her soil and enrich the farm environment for a diversity of birds. At the same time the business of farming requires marketing, pricing, transportation, waste management, and accounting. We are not likely to move effectively toward Earth restored by advocating only for natural capitalism or only for deep ecology. Resilient, sustainable adaptation is probably more subtle than any of our systems no matter how well thought out or deeply felt. Perhaps the rule to remember is "we make the road by walking." Can the natural capital approach and the deep ecology approach walk on parallel, or even overlapping roads toward Earth restored?

These approaches are potentially complementary. Both can have the well-being of the commonwealth of life in mind and can be based on an ecological understanding of the human-Earth relationship. Both can be informed by an ethic of "right relationship," which has a basis in ecological reality as we understand it.[17]

While there is clearly a tension between them we can draw on each in our quest for a new way to live on Earth. Modern science provides a context and the knowledge we need to guide the reshaping of the human-Earth relationship. While deep ecology is linked philosophically with ancient wisdom traditions, in modern times this perspective has been validated and enriched by the work of natural historians, geographers, wildlife biologists, geologists, geochemists, and cosmologists. Earth system science now gathers all this and more into a coherent story of how Earth has evolved and functions to support life. Deep ecology asserts that humans must understand and act in ways that are in harmony with essential elements of this story.

Natural capitalism, being a child of the modern monetized economy, does not link up with ancient wisdom in the same way. It emerged within the science of economics when some economists recognized that a huge factor of value and a major element of cost accounting were missing from conventional research and analysis. If natural capitalism is implemented within a context of respect for Creation and a commitment to restore a mutually enhancing human-Earth relationship, it offers an important toolkit for renewing and sustaining healthy ecosystems. Both deep ecology and natural capitalism understand the importance of turning to science for guidance in our quest to understand how to live on Earth without destroying it. In modern times, the assumptions, institutions, and practices of industrial capitalism have largely determined the nature of the human-Earth relationship. Natural capitalism has the potential to use some of these practices to ameliorate the ecological and social costs of the dominant paradigm. A deep ecology perspective has the potential to infuse the human-Earth relationship with reverence, respect, and gratitude for Earth's gifts and to help us live in greater harmony with how Earth's ecosystems actually work.

Our inquiry into these two perspectives has led us to a third—the underlying context of "the commons." The commons represents those resources or parts of Earth held in common and managed for the well-being of all. The natural capital argument that all Earth's resources and services, previously unvalued by the economy, should be valued and paid for by the market, is a recognition of the underlying commons on which economic life is built. In a similar way, the deep ecology argument that healthy ecosystems underwrite healthy human economies, is also a recognition of the underlying commons. The commons is the biophysical and social context in which human adaptation began, in which it has developed, and which continues to this very day to be the central factor from which economic activity continually emerges. But more than this, the commons is also built up out of economic and social activity.

We increase the domain and extent of the commons by human action. A very large part of economic and social life everywhere depends on the commons, often in a partly hidden way, but still, in many regions of the world, in an open cooperative way. The great potential of the commons as a vehicle for organizing and conducting the human economic enterprise is re-emerging into view. Reclaiming, revitalizing, and expanding the commons offers an avenue of development in which both natural capital and deep ecology can unfold their approaches to good effect. The commons approach to Earth restored could help shape a qualitatively different human-Earth relationship.

The Commons: A Bridge to the Future

In the showdown between the capital-driven economy and the integrity of Earth's ecosystems, a new and hopeful metaphor has emerged—"a bridge to the future."[18] If we want to save a reasonable fraction of the benefits of civilization, we have to save the economy as well, though that does not mean saving the economy in its present form. It means building a bridge to the future in which the economy supports biodiversity, ecosystem resilience, environmental justice, and the security and well-being of human communities—a whole Earth economy that works to the benefit of the whole commonwealth of life.

One promising bridge to the future is the re-emergence of the commons as a vehicle for helping insure that: (1) all people have right of access to the means of life that Earth provides; (2) these life-giving gifts are used more for the common good than for private wealth accumulation; (3) they are used in a way that secures this same right of access for future generations. This idea of the commons is more far-reaching

32

than the idea of setting aside national parks and other wilderness or scenic places for all to enjoy. It involves moving key resources essential to supporting life out of the marketplace into what Elinor Ostrom calls "common pool resources" to be governed by and for the benefit of users at local levels in an equitable and sustainable manner.[19]

While the commons are open to access by all, there are limits on the behavior of any one species in the commons. Creating these limits is not an easy process. When successful, managed commons allow for long-term sustainability without the constraints of markets and private property. Over the past century, some of the negative effects of the industrial revolution have been addressed from a commons point of view. The air has been cleared of some forms of pollution; reduction of acidic effluents has allowed some restoration of lakes and rivers so fish can live, and with protection some wild creatures have returned to our woodlands and skies. These are success stories for a managed commons.

The commons encompasses two domains: the cultural arrangements of knowledge and skills that support human communities, and the structures and processes of Earth's life support systems. Recognizing the reality of the commons in both domains offers the possibility of reconciling natural capitalism and deep ecology. The well-being of human communities, a main concern of natural capitalism, and the well-being of the commonwealth of life, a main concern of deep ecology, could both be goals of a managed commons. With the commons as a field of action the differences between these approaches need not hinder collaboration. The commons could be organized and managed to strengthen a sense of human solidarity and solidarity with Earth as a commonwealth of life.

Protecting and Renewing the Commons

Meanwhile, we are confronted with another reality. The ethic of competition, domination, and wealth accumulation is still seen by many as the best way to organize economic and social relationships. The goal of profit making above all else drives the large corporate structures that dominate our eco-

33

nomic and political life. The commons are increasingly vulnerable to expropriation by powerful corporate interests. Corporations roam the world seeking opportunities to advance wealth accumulation. This behavior recognizes no ecological limits on what it has the self-assigned "right" to take over and exploit for profit. For example, a transnational corporation was recently poised to acquire ninety percent of the arable land of Madagascar with no concern for the natural habitats of the island nation. Only a political rebellion against the President, who had signed the deal, stopped the land grab. Meanwhile, transnational corporations and foreign national interests, such as China and Korea, have been acquiring large tracts of agricultural and mineral-rich land in other parts of Africa.

Both the natural capital commons of Earth's life support systems and the cultural commons of knowledge and skills are seen as "resources" for exploitation and private wealth accumulation. Great inequity accompanies this exploitation, and leads to overt violence of emerging "resource wars." Transnational corporations and aggressive national interests are certainly aiming to "build a bridge to their future," but not one consistent with the preservation of the commons and the common good of all peoples and all life. The human prospect now includes the question, "will access to the means of life be increasingly controlled by a small number of corporate interests and their political allies, or will human communities, in all their variety, retain vital and resilient relationships to their local and regional environments?"

The way this great question is answered in the economic and political practice of communities around the world will determine, to a large extent, the fate of the commons and the quality of human life in the future. The dramatic overreach of corporate exploitation of the natural world and the world-wide response of indigenous and community-based cultures asserting their right to a physical/cultural commons, mark a turning point. This may be a new opening in the struggle for the commons and the practice of right relationship with respect to Earth.

Chapter 5
Property and the Commons

Though the Earth, and all its inferior Creatures be common to all Men, yet every Man has a property in his own Person. ... The Labour of his Body, and the Work of his hands, we may say, are properly his. ... Whatsoever then he removes out of the State that Nature hath provided, and left it in, he hath mixed his Labour with, and joined to it something that is his own, and thereby makes it his Property ... at least where there is enough, and as good left in common for others.

—John Locke[20]

The human use of Earth is now mediated almost entirely through the institution of property. The modern property regime started with the control of land, moved to intellectual and cultural activity, and is now attempting to enclose genetic structure and its expression. We are concerned here primarily with the control of land and its resources. In order to avoid cumbersome constructions, "land" will hereafter be used to denote the entire spectrum of ecosystem features that human activity appropriates for use.

The institution of property, and, in particular, private property, is one of the significant factors in the wealth-accumulating prowess of modern European and American political economies. However, political economies organized around maximizing wealth accumulation regularly degrade the life support capacity of Earth's ecosystems. The beneficial and progressive influence of private property has been exploited by the drive for wealth accumulation to the point where societal and ecological breakdown is now canceling out many of its benefits. Property sits squarely in the middle of our environmental and social crisis and is central to our quest for Earth restored. The path toward Earth restored is a path into understanding property and its relationship to natural capital, deep ecology, and the commons.

In the United States, private property is taken for granted; it has the status of natural law. But property is not a matter of natural law; it is a civic invention with a history of change in relation to knowledge and circumstance, and varies from culture to culture and from society to society.

All property rests on the commons and can be considered to exist only with reference to the commons. This may seem like an obvious statement, but in practice, especially in the United States, the reference is often deeply submerged or even lost. The land provided by Earth does not cease being a commons when persons obtain the opportunity to exercise control over it and use it. If anyone doubts this observation, a reading of the eye-opening book, *The World Without Us*, will settle the matter.[21] This book is a science-based account of how the planetary commons would respond if all human activity suddenly stopped. Objectively speaking, the commons is the ultimate arbiter of all forms of civilization, including property.

Where Did Property Come From?

How did the contemporary private property regime evolve to such wide control over land? The story of property in Western Civilization begins with Divine Right. In late 16th Century England Sir Robert Filmer[22] laid out the theological, political, and legal basis for the Divine Right of Monarchy over all lands. He reasoned that God owns the world and has given the control of his earthly estate to his proxy, the King. The King has full and absolute jurisdiction over all land and its creatures, and over all the people on the lands of the Kingdom. The King takes his oath to God alone and is subject only to God's laws. The King's edicts create and establish the law in human affairs, including the law of property. He can provide the rights of property to whomever he wishes. Filmer argued that the Monarchy was the supreme conduit of Divine

Authority in Earthly affairs. This is the power relationship in which the idea of property and the rights of property begin in the Anglo-American legal tradition.

In the 17th Century this political and legal philosophy became hugely contested. John Locke, along with others, provided the political philosophy of constitutional government that the politics of the time required.[23] Locke developed a line of reasoning that moved property authorization from the Divine Right of Kings to the responsibility of constitutional government. Locke reasoned that Earth, and its potential for supporting human life, had been given by God, not to the King and a hereditary Monarchy, but to all people in common without exception. Locke further reasoned that the right to hold property was legitimately acquired when men mixed their labor into land and resources. He further argued that the right to accumulate property has standing only if and when "there is enough, and as good left in common for others." Locke provided not only a credible alternative to the Monarch's Divine Right over land; he also insisted that equitable access to the means of life was a fundamental moral principle of constitutional governance. Locke's philosophy of political authority and governance replaced Filmer's and the Monarchy lost its grip. Unfortunately, while Locke's argument for constitutional governance of property carried the day, his moral framework of equitable access to the means of life did not find favor with those bent on wealth accumulation and empire.

In the early colonial era, for example, new lands were simply occupied in the name of the King. That was all it took to turn vast reaches of land into property; that, and the superior force of arms. As the Divine Right of Monarchy was muted by the authority of constitutional government, the acquisition and control of foreign lands migrated to civic administration. A vestige of Monarchical right was retained, however, in many cases where land was being turned into property by means of confiscation and outright theft with no pretense of aboriginal agreement. The invocation of the Crown, backed up with rifles, was a common short cut to property rights, first in New World jurisdictions, and then in worldwide empires.

With the colonial American rebellion against the English Monarch, property rights were cut off from this pretense of Divine Authority. John Locke's political philosophy was central to the concept of the new Republic and provided the basis for property rights to be developed entirely within a constitutional structure and civic process. Even here, however, the ghost of Divine Authority remained. First beyond the Appalachians, and then beyond the Mississippi, the policy of "Manifest Destiny" was (and still is) a stand-in for Divine Authority and the absolute right of the Monarch to convert land to property and dole it out to the faithful within a structure of investment and inheritance.[24] Ask almost any American landowner if they think they have an absolute right to their property, and they will say, "yes." If you ask where that right comes from they are likely to say something like, "I own it. It's mine!" There is a great and fierce reluctance to accept the fact that property is defined by government, and that the right to property and the control of property is a changing story according to relationships of power within various legal jurisdictions.

Where is Property Going?

After a substantial review of this history, historian of property law Eric Freyfogle writes:

> *"[T]he elements of ownership are set by history and experience, and we should look to our cultural traditions to see what ownership has come to mean. ... The problem here is that our history has become one of continuous change. There's no stable past that we can draw on. ... In the end, the only sensible grounding for property law is the one we've had all along. Property is a product of democratic governance. Today's lawmakers get to say what can be owned and what it means to own. ... With this legal grounding for private ownership in place we can add to it the principle philosophical justification to give property a moral grounding. ...*

"The central justification for landownership ... is overall social utility. This means we should craft individual rights and protect those rights to the extent that society as a whole is better off when we do so. ... [E]very landowner right must prove itself by its contribution to social utility."[25]

Freyfogle argues that in order to realize the very real benefits of private property, it must be understood in its underlying context of the commons.

"One reason why nineteenth-century ideas about landownership have come under attack, leading to a whole new generation of land-use laws, is that we are broadening our sense of moral value. We're sensing that, in some way, moral value extends beyond human life to encompass other life forms. ... There is a growing recognition, also, that people living today have obligations to take care of the land for future generations, perhaps to keep all life forms around for them to enjoy or use, perhaps to keep the land fertile, productive, and diverse. ...

"These new awarenesses are prompting us to see land anew. They also push us to revisit a question that property law has dealt with for centuries: what part of nature should pass into private hands and be considered private property, and what parts should instead remain subject to communal ownership or greater communal control? ...

"Seeing the world as we now do, should we broaden the list of lands that remain in public control or subject to special limitations? Instead, and more ambitiously, should we redefine what private landownership is about so we protect the public's interest in the ways all parts of nature are used? ...

"Perhaps we should embrace a notion that landowners are stewards, with clear rights to use but only limited rights to degrade and consume. Perhaps we need to apply more broadly the idea that all nature remains, in

a sense, in public hands, with private owners receiving only prescribed right to use."[26]

From this discussion we can understand that:

- the well-being of Earth's commonwealth is the moral basis of property;

- civic process establishes property and sets the rules that govern its use;

- the ecological world view expands the domain of values and ethics into the whole commonwealth of life; and

- the human-Earth relationship frames the stewardship ethic needed for guiding the sustainable use of Earth's ecosystems.

We are now ready to ask:

- How can a civic re-instatement and re-development of the commons approach integrate institutions of public trust under a stewardship ethic into a practical program for achieving Earth restored and equitable access to the means of life, for all peoples?

- How can the regime of private property, which now works disproportionately for the jurisdictions of wealth, team up in a balanced way with institutions of public trust, to advance the common good and the well-being of the whole commonwealth of life?

The natural capital and the deep ecology approaches both have a great stake in answering these questions. To find the answers, both approaches find their way into a context of the commons that puts property on a new footing and the human-Earth relationship on the path to restoration. On that path, one natural resource that needs serious attention is water, a prime example of the conflict between private property and the commons.

Chapter 6
Water: Essential, Yet Threatened

If the wars of this century were fought over oil, the wars of the next century will be fought over water.

—Ismail Serageldin (1995)[27]

Life on Earth is not possible without water. Humans are two-thirds water, and so are all the other living creatures. We live on the blue planet, the surface of which is mostly water. But most (97.3%) of the water on Earth is in our oceans and salty groundwater. And most of the fresh water is in glaciers (1.8%) and groundwater (0.8%), which leaves only 0.1% of the total water as accessible fresh surface water in rivers, lakes and wetlands.[28]

Water is the ultimate renewable resource, an essential part of the commons. Water in rivers, wetlands, lakes, seas oceans, and underground is renewable through the hydrologic cycle. Energy from the sun causes surface water to evaporate and plants give off water during transpiration, both of which produce clouds. As air masses are transported around Earth, they cool enough that the water vapor condenses and falls back to Earth as rain, snow, sleet, or hail. That which seeps into the ground re-charges the groundwater. Some runs off into wetlands, lakes, streams, rivers, and, eventually to the oceans. This is the natural process uninterrupted by human activities.

But the living creatures on Earth are running out of clean fresh water because humans have polluted, diverted and depleted the available fresh water. Sources of pollution include organic wastes from the growth of our food, chemical wastes from industrial production of all the things we use,

41

chemical and thermal pollution from production of energy for our activities, and our own waste in the form of sewage, garbage, and trash.

Sources of water are not necessarily where the human need for water occurs. Major cities such as Los Angeles and Las Vegas built on deserts confront increasing problems of water scarcity as they expand even further. So much water is diverted through huge piping systems or bottled for sale. Dams interrupt the natural flow of rivers making large reservoirs for water supply and the generation of electricity. Groundwater is being depleted because it is pumped at rates greater than the natural re-charge rate. Major rivers no longer flow to the sea because the water is diverted, producing dry riverbeds and dry deltas. In 2010 humans appropriated half of all freshwater flows for their use.[29]

Fresh water is essential for life and must be available, not only for human use, but for all the other creatures on Earth. Wars are currently being fought over oil, but as we deplete and pollute Earth's freshwater and the human population continues to increase, the world's conflicts will be over water. While we have alternative sources of energy that we can use as oil runs out, there is no alternative to water.

Who Owns Water?

So God created man in his own image, in the image of God created he him; male and female created he them. And God blessed them, and God said unto them, Be fruitful, and multiply, and replenish Earth, and subdue it; and have dominion over the fish of the sea, and over the fowl of the air, and over every living thing that moveth upon Earth.

—*Genesis* 1:27-28 (King James)

From these words the Europeans and their descendents derive their concept of ownership and dominion. As we ponder the effect of this injunction, and try to gain perspective on its influence in the development of Western Civilization, it helps to pause and realize that indigenous cultures have no such ownership concept, but instead consider nature sacred and its gifts to be forever shared.

Every part of this soil is sacred in the estimation of my people. Every hillside, every valley, every plain and grove, has been hallowed by some sad or happy event in days long vanished.[30]

This world view reminds us that through the attitude of respect and sharing, the values of cooperation and reciprocity, and in legal agreements, the commons can become a bridge to the future.

Under the Western ownership and dominion concept, water law developed two distinct systems in the United States. In the early settlement of the eastern U.S., land taken from the Native Americans was designated as private property. There were abundant streams and rivers. Consequently, a system of water law developed considering the owners of water rights to be the owners of land bordering a waterway, called "riparian" rights, which means "that lying adjacent to a stream, river, pond or small lake." The natural flow rule was that every land owner had the right for water to flow past their land undiminished in quality or quantity. Each riparian land owner had the right of "reasonable use" as long as it did not deprive the rights of those downstream. If there was an insufficient quantity available, all must reduce their use in proportion to the amount of their privately owned land. This meant that the European settlers who occupied land next to a river and eventually became owners of the land under the colonial and later national systems were the ones who had the right to the water in that river. Where were the rights of indigenous peoples who first occupied that land?[31]

But in the western U.S., water was scarce and public lands were used for private purposes such as grazing and mining. A system of "prior appropriation" developed. The principles were "first in time, first in right" and "beneficial use." That meant that whoever first used the water in a particular area had the first right to it, assuming that use could be deemed beneficial. Many states have evolved to a permit system to enforce the prior appropriation system. Some states have systems that include both riparian and prior appropriation aspects. But these European settlers were not the first to use the water; the indigenous people were there first. And none of these systems of law considers the needs of other creatures for water.

Water quality in the U.S. is covered by the Clean Water Act. Originally enacted as the Federal Water Pollution Control Act in 1948, it took its current form with major amendments in 1972. The Act includes general water quality standards, effluent standards for particular industries, a discharge permit program, a construction loan program for public water treatment facilites, and provisions for special problems like toxic chemical or oil spills. Major amendments have been made to the Act in 1977 and 1987. Groundwater is not covered by the Clean Water Act.

Because of the interconnectivity of groundwater systems (aquifers) and the difficulties of assessing the quantity that is available and how much has been removed, the issue of who has rights to groundwater is more complex. In the U.S. groundwater has generally been pumped without limits. In some legal cases groundwater has been considered as a non-renewable resource as if it were being mined. Some riparian rights have been allowed, giving absolute ownership of water underlying owned land. Some prior appropriation rights have been given to the first pumper of groundwater in an area. Groundwater quality is covered in the U.S. in the Safe Drinking Water Act, Resource Conservation and Recovery Act, and the Superfund clean-up program.

At the international level, the "law of trans-boundary aquifers," was adopted by the United Nations General Assembly on January 15, 2009. Following the principles of equitable and reasonable utilization, and no harm, the resolution delineates all the factors that must be considered in the development of utilization plans, indicates that long-term benefits must be maximized, and emphasizes that an aquifer shall not be utilized in a way "that would prevent continuance of its effective functioning."[32]

Water: Commons or Commodity

In most of European and in North American cities, systems of public water supply and sewage disposal developed in the nineteenth century for the protection of public health, and most of these systems continue to provide public services today. However, at the same time in France a private water industry developed around two major companies that have now evolved into the two most powerful transnational water corporations, Suez and Veolia. In 1989 Britain privatized their water systems, which led to the third largest water corporation, British-German RWE Thames.[33]

Lacking in resources, developing countries were slower to develop water supply and sanitation systems to serve all their people. Acknowledging this growing problem, the U.N. declared the decade of the 1980s as the International Drinking Water and Sanitation Decade and the International Monetary Fund (IMF) and the World Bank (WB) encouraged the development of public water and sewage systems. But by the 1990s the IMF and WB had adopted what has been called "the Washington Consensus," a financial reform prescription for developing countries based upon privatization of public services, including water supply and sanitation. This has been imposed upon impoverished, developing countries by the WB and IMF. International water organizations have been developed, the Global Water Partnership and the World Water Council, but they are dominated by the major water and other corporations. International water policy is set at the meetings of these organizations, which furthers the goal of privatization of developing countries' water systems.

Privatization of water supplies is another extension of the concept of private ownership of property. In order to re-negotiate their large debt burdens, developing countries have been required to sell their public water supply system to the highest bidder, usually to a large international corporation. These corporations then expect to earn a profit supplying water. Millions of women spend hours each day walking long distances and standing in long lines to get water for their families. Privatization of water systems has only made this worse as people cannot afford to pay the prices charged for water.

In Cochabamba, Bolivia, the people fought back against privatization of their water system. In 1998 the Bechtel Corporation took over that city's water supply and the price tripled. Those who could not pay were cut off. It took two years of demonstrations in which one person was killed, but eventually the Bolivian government cancelled the contract with Bechtel. Other communities in South America and across the world have resisted the privatization of their water supplies. But even where the people can afford the higher prices, such as in the United States, privatization of water systems have not worked. Many contracts have been cancelled citing broken promises, dirty water, and faulty infrastructure.

Transforming water into yet another private property resource shows the irrationality of continuing down our current path of wealth creation through commoditization of resources. Instead of increasing the viability of all species that depend on clean water, using the current private property regime only locks up the remaining pure water for those humans with enough money to pay its price. When water is returned to the commons, its importance as a source of all life can be recognized and its role as a portion of the natural capital of the economic system can be measured and equitably allocated.

Human Right to Clean Fresh Water

Is access to clean, fresh water a human right? Water was not included in the original 1947 U. N. Universal Declaration of Human Rights, but there are now calls for a "right to water" convention to be adopted at the U.N. Right to water has been included in several proposed U.N. General Assembly and Committee Resolutions since 2000. Finally, on July 28th, 2010, the U.N. General Assembly voted unanimously, with 124 nations in favor and 42 abstentions, for a resolution that declared water and sanitation to be human rights. The U.S. and Canada were among the countries abstaining, presumably because they are concerned about their obligations should they be required to provide clean, fresh water to all their citizens. This non-binding resolution is just a first step because there are no provisions for enforcement.[34]

Natural Capital Approach to Water

The economy today has a huge appetite for water: farmers rely on massive irrigation for their crops, energy production uses huge amounts of water for cooling, industry uses vast amounts of water in production processes, and urban dwellers consume water in large quantities. As rain falls from the sky, flows in our rivers, collects in aquifers and lakes and, finally, settles in our great oceans, it is part of the biotic process; but as the economy makes demands on these flows of water, the natural system becomes severely imbalanced.

We have been treating water as a free resource because it was available for the taking. People with the financial muscle have been staking out private claims on this resource. It is being transformed into a private commodity and its characteristic in the commons as a natural right of all living beings is disappearing.

As fresh water becomes more scarce relative to the demands for its use in an industrial society, it is becoming clearer that it is anything but free. It is no longer simply a part of the natural ecosystem; it has become, whether we like it or not, a semi-renewable form of natural capital, one which cannot be used sustainably unless it is made to follow the rules of real capital. Paradoxically, building new economic structures that will limit the destructive use of natural systems introduces a contradiction. Suddenly part of the world that has traditionally been managed by physical and biological systems is falling more and more under the management of the economic system.

What would be the natural capital approach to the management of water on Earth? It is impossible to go back in time. We must deal with the world as it is today. It is a world where all forms of water are used to excess relative to naturally occurring regeneration systems, so it has become imperative to limit water usage. We may need to establish an

47

infrastructure for water capital, complete with agencies and community organizations that decide who gets how much water when. More controversially, the use of water must be priced. Wealth, power and prices result in allocations that are not necessarily (or easily) based on equity. Economic investment goods tend to go to those with wealth and power. We do not want that to happen with water—a common good that is critical to sustaining life for all living creatures.

For Quakers and all others who value equity among peoples, the spirit that is brought to the design of a water capital system is of utmost importance. Before agreement on technical and legal details, the realities of human feelings, values, and interests will be on the agenda. Why do people feel the way they do about their use of water? Everyone is likely to resist a realistic pricing of water. Households will think, "if this decision is made regarding water, I will have less money, and my way of life will be harmed." Corporation leaders will think, "if water is priced, I will be less able to make money and my business will be harmed." Unless that reaction is addressed, there is little chance of finding a unity that reflects the needs of all biotic systems. It is important to recognize how such points of view inform the range of policy choices people find acceptable in addressing water issues.

Deep Ecology Approach to Water

What would be the deep ecology approach to the management of water on Earth? If water is becoming scarce, it is because the economy has a huge appetite for water. But we distance ourselves from the problem when we say it is the economy that has a huge appetite for water. It is we humans who have a profligate thirst for water and the wealth that water can bring. It is we humans who have forgotten that water is an essential source of life on Earth to be cherished and shared with all other life forms. If we want future generations of any species to survive and thrive on this planet, we have no choice but to stop desecrating and wasting water and begin protecting this sacred source of life.

While it may not be possible to return to a low population freely accessing plentiful sources of fresh water, it is possible to advance and build up an approach to human settlement and water use guided by ecological resilience and sustainability. Rather than simply pricing water within the market system, the deep ecology approach looks first to the relationships of human settlements and economic activity—the total design of adaptation—within the hydrologic reality of specific ecosystems and Earth's ecosystem as a whole.

Here again, we see the fundamental question: should the focus be on managing Earth or on managing ourselves? Looking at human history since the beginning of the Industrial Revolution, and considering the outcome, we might say we have had a good long run at managing Earth and the results are looking more and more grim not only for our species, but for the whole commonwealth of life. If the human enterprise has any chance of pulling itself out of this ecologically destructive mode of adaptation, we will have to rapidly shift from Earth management to self-management.

Pricing access to water may well be an important tool in the self-management of human settlements and economic activity, but without a complete reorientation to human adaptation, guided by the deep ecology approach, it could end up as just a way of rationing a depleting resource and negotiating the rate of depletion. Pricing alone, as noted above, will likely just favor the survival of the wealthy. The deep ecology approach insists that we must cross over from negotiating the rate of depletion to conserving and living within the rate of replenishment.

The deep ecology approach takes the knowledge of earth system science as a guide and the ecologically sound adaptation of human settlements to the realities of various ecosystems as a strategy, and thus aims for a mutually enhancing human-Earth relationship. Equitable access to the means of life, including water, will be likely only if full cost accounting is set within an ethical framework of reciprocity, stewardship, and cooperation, in short, within the framework of the integrity of the commons.

Society-wide Governance

With this comparison and contrast of the natural capital and deep ecology approaches to water, we come to another central question: How should the human community govern the use of water? Should the market system, in which the pricing of natural capital fits, be seen as a system of society-wide governance? Many economists and public policy professionals will say, "Yes, it's the best system of governance we have." Earth system scientists, ecological economists, and many ethicists will say the market system should not be seen, or made to operate, as a society-wide system of governance. At its best, the market system is a kind of tool kit with pricing and full cost accounting among its best tools, but society-wide governance, and especially the governance of Earth's resources and access to the means of life, is a political, cultural, ethical, and even spiritual decision-making process.

The deep ecology approach might be blended with a carefully tailored application of natural capital pricing and market allocation of water and other resources if it is within a system of values and governance that starts with a basic commitment to the health and resilience of the whole commonwealth of life. This again brings us to the reality of the commons, the question of the human-Earth relationship, and the creation of the kind of governance that will build resilient and sustainable adaptation.

From this discussion we can understand that:

- Water is essential for life; there is no substitute.

- Only 0.1% of the water on Earth is surface freshwater available for use by the creatures who live on this planet, including humans.

- Conflicts over water in the eastern U.S. have been settled in courts based on riparian rights, the right of those living along a stream or river to reasonable water use that does not deprive those downstream of the quantity or quality of water they need.

- In the western U.S. water rights have been based upon a first use, beneficial use principle in which the first European settlers to use the water had the right to it as long as the use was a beneficial one.

- Water is not always located in the same areas where human populations are, so much water is diverted to cities.

- Groundwater has been pumped in the U.S., mostly without control and aquifers are being depleted.

- In developing countries it is generally the woman's role to walk sometimes miles, stand in line, and wait to obtain water for her family's needs.

- Water is increasingly being privatized, considered a commodity to be owned and sold, often at a price too high for many households' resources.

- Global policies concerning the distribution of water on Earth are being decided at conferences of global organizations dominated by international water and other corporations.

- While water was not included in the 1947 United Nations Declaration of Human Rights, a resolution was passed in the 2010 United Nations General Assembly that declared water and sanitation to be human rights.

We are now ready to ask:

- How can the natural capital approach be used to bring water distribution into an equitable and sustainable system?

- How can the deep ecology approach be used to consider not only the human need for water, but the function of water throughout the entire biosphere upon which all the creatures of Earth depend for life?

- How can water be brought under management as a common resource for the benefit of all?

Chapter 7
Governing the Commons

The tragedy of the commons develops in this way. Picture a pasture open to all. It is to be expected that each herdsman will try to keep as many cattle as possible on the commons. ... Each man is locked into a system that compels him to increase his herd without limit—in a world that is limited. Ruin is the destination toward which all men rush, each pursuing his own best interest in a society that believes in the freedom of the commons. Freedom in a commons brings ruin to all.

—Garrett Hardin[35]

The commons got a bad reputation when the phrase, "the tragedy of the commons," was used in a 1968 essay by Garrett Hardin.[35] His pessimistic assessment, quoted above, was quickly picked up by those who wanted to see the end of the commons as proof that private property was the only way to handle resources responsibly. This was not Hardin's point. He was arguing that in the circumstance of increasing population, an unregulated commons will be destroyed. While he allowed that private property could have a positive role in managing resources, he saw that government regulation was required to preserve the commons. His analysis was also framed within the assumption of behavior driven entirely by shortsighted self-interest. Hardin was mainly concerned to make a strong point about the need for regulation of resources with respect to population growth. Unfortunately, he overlooked a long history of commons that are managed wisely by community-based organizations.

Even before Hardin's essay was published, Ostrom (1965)[36] had studied the development of self-governing public enterprises for management of groundwater in Los Angeles. For over four decades she and her colleagues have amassed a large number of studies of both successful and unsuccessful cases of commons governance. For this work she was awarded the Nobel Prize in Economics in 2009.[37]

High-Mountain Grazing and Forest Lands

In her book, *Governing the Commons: The Evolution of Institutions for Collective Action*, Ostrom[38] describes successful and failed community-based, self-governing institutions for management of the commons, as well as attempts to change existing institutions. The successful long-enduring institutions included high-mountain grazing and forestland management in Switzerland and Japan, as well as irrigation societies in Spain and the Philippines. The first written rules for the use of the commonly owned mountain slopes for summer grazing of cattle and use of timber in Töbel, Switzerland, were dated in the year 1224 and a document of agreement was signed by all the residents in 1483. These agreements are truly long-enduring as they have persisted through the generations ever since.

A similar situation exists in Japan where villages govern the high mountain slopes. As much as twelve million hectares were governed by villages between 1600 and 1867, and three million hectares continue to be managed in this way today with no evident ecological damage.

Distribution of Irrigation Water

In Valencia, Spain, rules for distribution of water for irrigation were developed before 1238 and written out in 1435 when 84 residents met and approved regulations covering who had rights to the water, how it would be shared in good years and bad, how the canals would be maintained, how they would elect officials, and how they would enforce the regulations with fines. For over 500 years farmers have met, elected officials, and revised the rules when necessary.

In the Philippines the written records of irrigation agreements date back to notes from Spanish priests in 1630, but the practice was well developed at that time. In 1979 there were 686 such communal irrigation systems in one small province, Ilocos Norte, in the Philippines.

Design Principles

From these and other case studies, Ostrom and her colleagues[39] developed eight "design principles" for successful self-governing organizations to manage the commons:

1) Clearly defined boundaries, both of the commons and of the users;

2) Congruence between the local conditions and the rules that restrict time, place, technology, and quantity of use;

3) Participation of those most affected in modification of the rules;

4) Monitoring by the users or those accountable to the users;

5) Sanctions and punishments graduated by the seriousness of the offense and the context with allowances for emergency situations;

6) Rapid access to low-cost conflict resolution services;

7) Right to organize not challenged by the external government; and

8) Nested enterprises for commons that are parts of larger systems.

Creation of Self-governing Institutions

Since the long-enduring institutions provided no opportunity for investigation of the process of development of the institutions, the groundwater situation in Los Angeles was analyzed as an example of development of contemporary self-governed institutions. This situation involved several inter-connected groundwater basins serving millions of people, many institutions competing for access to the water, and 16 years of agreement-stabilizing negotiation and litigation. The solution was not one centralized, controlling entity, but a multi-agency "replenishment district" that would be responsible for repelling saltwater intrusion in the fresh groundwater, recharging the groundwater, and reducing the pumping from groundwater to safe levels that did not deplete the supply beyond that which was recharged. The Central and West Basin Water Replenishment District was created by the water suppliers and approved by the citizens living in the area with the power to tax, sue and provide water. Control of the system is by a court-appointed watermaster service provided by the State of California. The watermaster calibrates all meters and conducts all the monitoring. It is not necessary for the watermaster to enforce any of the rules. The information from monitoring is merely provided to all the participants. If any one of the agencies violates the rules, the others take care of the problem by persuasion or litigation.[40]

Situations where self-governing institutions were tried and failed were also studied. A successful cooperative among one set of fishers was formed in Alanya, Turkey, but two other attempts at fishing cooperatives in Turkey failed. In those that failed, a wide variety of sizes of boats and technologies were used, from small-scale fishers to large-scale trawlers, so conflicts between the groups made it difficult to establish rules that would apply to all. The coast guard and local police were supposed to enforce the rules, but did not have the resources or the motivation to do so. Finally, the political setting did not provide low-cost support for conflict resolution.

Self-governing institutions are developed when unorganized individuals decide to organize into an institution operating under a set of rules that forbid, require, or permit actions. The process for creating or changing the rules must involve all the participants.

Cooperative agreement on the governance of the commons is key to resource management based on either a natural capital or deep ecology approach. As noted in the case studies of commons presented above, the management of resources for future sustainability cannot be achieved without major changes in the way society conceptualizes economic property rules.

Governing Complex
Regional and Global Commons

The Ostrom group[41] has also conducted studies of the management of regional or global commons, which show that no one model of governance is successful in all situations. Private ownership, government intervention, and community institutions all have their place. But community-based groups and traditional tools are often ignored in the development of environmental policy. They defined four kinds of capital:

1) Natural capital is Earth's resources available for human exploitation.

2) Physical capital is the stock of human-made material resources that can be used to produce a flow of future income.

3) Human capital is the acquired knowledge and skills that an individual brings to an activity.

4) Social capital is the set of rules and norms underlying social behavior and order that represents particular forms of organization in society.

The studies show the importance of social capital in developing trust, reciprocity, and networks of civic engagement, all of which are important to developing the rules and laws that function to govern the commons in situations of complexity.

One major challenge for governing the commons is accurate, reliable information on the resource stocks, flow of usage, and the processes involved. For large, complex situations, it is important to get the scale of monitoring correct. Information can be too general, which averages out important local variations; or it can be too specific, so that the crucial information is lost in too much detail. Decision-makers also need to know the uncertainty in the information. Since every environmental decision balances various trade-offs, information about individual and social values are needed.

Conflict is inevitable in complex management situations because resource management includes parties that come with very different interests, value systems, and power. Strategies for conflict resolution include ballots or polls in which the parties have little interaction, adversarial systems with legal action, or mediated intense negotiating face-to-face sessions.

Enforcement of the rules agreed upon with a level of tolerance for minor infractions is also important in complex situations. Those enforcing the rules must be seen as legitmate and effective or the system will break down. For regional or global situations, financial instruments may be used as an incentive for compliance. For example, tradeable environmental allowances (TEAs) can be used to limit withdrawals of a resource such as groundwater, or emssions, such as carbon. TEAs and community-based systems may have opposite strengths and weaknesses, so it is suggested that a combination of those two approaches might be used.

Also important in management of resources is infrastructure, which can determine the extent to which a resource can be exploited. Effective communication and roads may be a determining factor in complex situations involving local, regional and global systems. Institutional infrastructure provides for the research and social capital needed for effective management at multiple levels. Successful management systems are flexible, that is, they have mechanisms in place to make changes as needed.

Atmosphere as Commons

In his book, *Who Owns the Sky? Our Common Assets and the Future of Capitalism*,[42] Peter Barnes describes a public trust that operates independently of government and the market, a Sky Trust. This public trust institution would manage the atmosphere for its "owners"—all people. It would be chartered and mandated with legally binding fiduciary and environmental responsibility to price and manage the use that is made of the atmosphere resource in a way that drives down carbon emissions. Barnes shows how a Sky Trust, and other similar public trust institutions, could provide the new operating system needed by the market to prevent capitalism from destroying Earth's common pool resources and itself in the process. In a second book, *Capitalism 3.0: A Guide to Reclaiming the Commons*,[43] he extends the public trust concept to the whole range of the commons. Out of this comes a domain of public trusteeships based on the moral obligation and ecological wisdom of preserving the gifts of Creation, and which are set up in a way that helps provide equitable access to the means of life for all people.

Kerala and Mondragon: Cooperative Examples

The two examples of Kerala[44] and Mondragon[45] show what is possible for human communities that put a high value on the common good and organize self-governing institutions to utilize their common resources to achieve good lives for everyone in their jurisdictions. Kerala is a state in southern India that by Western standards is impoverished, and Mondragon is a family of cooperative enterprises in northern Spain that has created a relatively prosperous regional social economy. The contrast between the two provides a strong argument for the wide applicability of the commons approach to the cooperative management of resources.

Kerala was once not only impoverished, but blighted by a particularly oppressive version of India's social caste system. Extreme inequality and economic exploitation ruled. Then, under the enlightened leadership of a number of figures, a social and political process began that eventually transformed Kerala into one of the most democratic and equitable societies in the world today. By agreeing to utilize their common resources—their physical and social capital—in a cooperative and equitable way, the people of Kerala have achieved a stunning result: a demographic profile that almost parallels the U.S. on one-seventieth of the income. Kerala still ranks in the poverty zone when measured by per capita income or Gross Domestic Product (GDP), but it ranks in the 88th percentile when measured on the Physical Quality of Life Index (PQLI), which is comparable to South Korea and Taiwan. The people of Kerala have proved that a high level of social development and community security does not depend on a high level of economic development. It depends on placing the values of the common good at the center of political process, and the techniques of cooperation at the center of decision-making on the use of resources.

The roots of the Mondragon phenomenon go back to the late 1940's when Don José Maria Arrizmendiarrieta, a Catholic pastor, established a technical training school and began to promote the idea of a cooperative, worker-owned enterprise. In 1956 six of his students established a stove manufacturing shop in the village of Mondragon. Additional cooperative businesses in a variety of manufacturing, agricultural, and service areas were soon added and flourished. The Mondragon Cooperative Corporation (MCC) is now a multi-billion dollar complex of linked worker/member-owned business, service and education enterprises employing over 30,000 people. A key factor ensuring the success of this cooperative approach to managing common capital resources was the establishment of a credit union, the Caja Laboral Popular or Community Bank. With this control of their financial resources, money management became an exercise in advancing the common good. Within the context of MCC, money became a public trust commons and a tool for supporting the best interests of all worker/members and their families.

Mondragon has proven that cooperative ownership and management of common resources is a viable alternative economic system to capitalism, even in the context of high technology manufacturing, and international trade, at which MCC excels. The key is not scale, level of technology, the kind of resources involved, or zone of development. The key lies in the design principles above as identified by Elinor Ostrom, and in the development of a social-political context that works to put them into effect for the common good.

59

Chapter 8
Human Nature in Earth Restored

Human communities are only as healthy as our conceptions of human nature.

—Dacher Keltner[46]

Governing the commons in the ways suggested above involves a new understanding of what it means for humans to live in right relationship with each other and with the larger commonwealth of life on Earth. As Elinor Ostrom's work suggests, managing the commons involves many challenges. We are proposing a significant expansion in the scope and reach of the commons as a pathway to a more sustainable way to live on Earth. Governing a common resource that functions effectively beyond the local level and incorporates the twin goals of sustaining both ecological integrity and social fairness is, indeed, an ambitious undertaking. It will require human participation at an unprecendented level of social and economic complexity. If we are to participate in ways that promote our own survival and that of the rest of the web of life, we will have to imagine a future very different from the present. We will have to respect and train our human capacities to be concerned for the greater good and make cooperation, collaboration and peaceful resolution of conflicts our default responses to problems that arise on our journey into a livable future.

In terms of surviving and thriving as a species, we humans can be seen to be very successful. Beginning some seven million years ago with a line of primates that led to the genus *Homo* and continuing up to and beyond the appearance of anatomically modern humans about 200,000 years ago, our ancestors lived in enough harmony with each other and with the natural world to enable our line to continue and to eventually grow in size and strength to populate all parts of the planet. Despite this record of success, we now face the possibility that the very size and power of our species may be our undoing and may lead to the unravelling of the web of life on Earth. To avoid this fate, it seems imperative to understand anew how to live in right relationship and to cultivate human qualities and societal institutions that encourage and enable us to live this way.

Is humanity up to these challenges? How we answer that question depends a lot on how we think about human nature. From archeology, anthropology and history we know that how human societies are organized varies tremendously over time and place. This variety of cultural expression is shaped by demands of survival and opportunities posed by the physical environment in which a culture develops. But beyond these fundamental shaping forces, cultures seem to select from a large menu of human propensities and behaviors a subset of culturally sanctioned qualities deemed necessary to meet human needs. They then cultivate these qualities through their spiritual beliefs and practices, and other cultural institutions. There seems to be a random and unconscious aspect to the particular subset of qualities that are emphasized in a given culture. For example, why does one culture decide that one's lineage is determined through the mother's line and another through the father's line? Who in the culture gets to make decisions like this? Whose interests are served by such choices?

What is the subset of human qualities that are currently favored in the culture of the U.S.? Jeremy Rifkin[47] points out that more than two centuries ago, when modern market economies and nation states were emerging in the West, Enlightenment philosophers such as John Locke, Adam Smith, Rene Descartes and others believed humans were materialistic, self-interested, competitive, rational, autonomous, independent, self-sufficient, and driven by a biological urge to be propertied and sovereign over their own domain. This picture of human beings held a promise of hope and improved the quality of life for many people whose lives were constrained under the yoke of the feudal system and it fed many of the assumptions on which free-market capitalism was built.

As Rifkin notes, this idea of human nature was a liberating step forward over the dark and fatalistic beliefs that prevailed in the West during the feudal and medieval periods. In those times the Christian Church taught that babies are born in sin and that personal salvation can only be found through Christ and in the next world. Indeed, in many places within the Church one finds echoes of these teachings today. This pessimistic view of human nature was instrumental in helping the Church maintain its power. It also helped to justify the need for Kings with their armies and land-owning aristocracies with their indentured labor to keep in check the unruly and immoral masses.

The view of human nature that emerged in the 18th century, and the political, economic and social institutions it fostered, have indeed led to important advances in material well-being and freedom for great numbers of people. However, at the beginning of the 21st century it is all too apparent that we must now reckon with the costs of these advances to us as social beings and to the planet's ecological health and integrity. We are at a critical turning point in understanding who we are as a species and our place in the larger community of life on Earth.

We are beginning to realize that the Enlightenment view of human nature is dangerously limited because it denigrates and even ignores the inherent relational and social needs and behavior of humans. It exalts the individual and blinds us to the negative consequences our actions may have on others— at personal, societal and planetary levels. Perhaps this partial view has run its course and it is now time to embrace a more comprehensive, balanced and, therefore, more accurate understanding of human nature.

The human and planetary story that unfolded in the 19th and 20th centuries should give us pause when considering what aspects of human nature we might want to cultivate and empower in the times ahead. Not only did we in the West elevate and reward human behaviors associated with self-interest, autonomy, individualism and materialism, we revved up the reach and intensity of these behaviors by using fossil fuels to run the human enterprise. It is as if we pumped up competitiveness, selfishness, consumerism and greed with steroids only to discover later how destructive this "performance enhancement" has been to personal, societal and ecological health and viability.

Dacher Keltner points out that "it has long been assumed that selfishness, greed, and competitiveness lie at the core of human behavior, the products of our evolution. It takes little imagination to see how these assumptions have guided most realms of human affairs, from policy making to media portrayals of social life."[48]

The good news is that recent scientific findings from many fields are forcefully challenging this one-sided view of human nature.

The Primacy of Cooperation and Empathy

We are social animals who depend on each other for life and well-being. The primate family to which humans belong includes species that have lived in social groups through millions of years of evolution including our closest genetic relatives, modern-day chimpanzees and bonobos. It is thought that some seven million years ago the line of primates leading to the genus *Homo* split off from the line leading to chimps and bonobos. Research by Sarah Blaffer Hrdy suggests that, "as long as a million and a half years ago, the African ancestors of *Homo sapiens* were already emotionally very different from the ancestors of any other extant ape "and that much of this difference was due to how our ancestors reared their offspring in a pattern called 'cooperative breeding.'"[49] Simply put this means that among our *Homo* ancestors, children were cared for and provisioned by many other members of the group in addition to the mother. This cooperative child-raising continued for the long period of time before these children could fend for themselves. This is in sharp contrast to most other primate mothers who do not trust others to care for their young.

Hrdy points out that, with many helpers, mothers can "devote energy to producing more and bigger babies..." and their children, "have the luxury of growing up slowly, building stronger bodies, better immune systems, and in some cases bigger brains..."[50] Hrdy makes the case that in this pattern of child-rearing we discover the roots of "empathy and mind reading in humans," a potent combination of abilities without which, "we would not have evolved to be human at all."[51] Hrdy's findings point to cooperation as a fundamental driver of human evolution and the context in which our capacity for empathy arises. It is within the framework of cooperative child-rearing where we first experience the feelings and emotions that allow us to develop empathic bonds and become fully mature social beings. As Rifkin notes, "Without feelings and emotions, empathy ceases to exist. A world without empathy is alien to the very notion of what a human being is."[52]

Since the early 1990s, neuroscientists and others have been studying "mirror neurons" in our brains to understand the biological mechanisms of our ability to empathize. These neurons allow humans to grasp the minds of others as if their thoughts and behaviors were their own through direct simulation—by feeling not by thinking. Mirror neuron circuitry is first activated by parental and community nurture of infants and as this nurture occurs, empathic pathways are established in the brain. Rifkin says that "The discovery of mirror neurons ... opens the door to exploring the biological mechanisms that make sociability possible."[53] Researchers in diverse disciplines are positing that "participation with the other ... the ability to read and respond to another person 'as if' he or she were oneself is the key to how human beings engage the world, create individual identity, develop language, learn to reason, become social, establish cultural narratives, and define reality and existence."[54] Rifkin suggests that many scientists working in this new field believe these findings point the way toward understanding how nature and nurture interact to create human nature.

Relationship:
The Crucible of Human Development

We humans have a large social brain that is hardwired for relationship. Shelley Taylor notes in her book, *The Tending Instinct,* that early theories about what drove development of our social brain

> *"... characterized man [sic] as aggressive and self-serving, manipulating the social environment for personal garnering of resources at the expense of others. Scientists have placed a lot of emphasis on the needs for tactical deception, misrepresentation, lying and other techniques of social control as prominent among the skills that the big brain affords. ... The male tasks around which social brain explanations were crafted—hunting, forming coalitions to defend against enemies, and luring potential mates away from competitors—are well served by outsmarting and deceiving others, and so such tactical skills may, for these reasons, have loomed large in early scientific accounts of the social brain."* [55]

She wryly points out that while these skills may be important for survival, "it is unlikely that the brain would have evolved primarily to furnish tactics of deception and manipulation. If so, we might well have tactically skewered one another right out of existence. By ignoring the kinder side of social life, we are left with, you might say, half a brain."[56] And, perhaps, less than half a picture of human nature.

We now know from research on the evolution and functioning of the social brain that nurturing experiences in life, such as the parent-child bond, cooperation, and other benign social relating are critical drivers of brain development and are essential to our success as a species. As Taylor notes, the ability to cooperate and to promote social harmony are survival assets. If you avoid war you are more likely to survive

65

to reproduce, than if you win it. Taylor's work has shown that the "flight or fight" response is only one way humans respond to stress. She draws on biology, evolutionary psychology, physiology and neuroscience to show that humans, particularly females, respond to stress by what she calls "tending and befriending."[57]

From an evolutionary perspective, tending—quieting and caring for offspring and blending into the environment—increases chances of survival. However, protecting oneself and one's children at the same time is no easy task, so females who could draw effectively on the social group for help—befriending—increased their own and their offspring's chances of survival. She argues that our big social brain has developed, not just because of the requirements of hunting and self-defense, but also because of the requirements of tending to others' needs and to getting one's own needs met by others.

Our sense of who we are—our very identity—develops only in relationship. Rifkin quotes Mikhail Bakhtin writing in 1984, "To *be* means to *communicate*...To be means to be for another, and through the other, for oneself. A person has no internal sovereign territory; he is wholly and always on the boundary, looking inside himself; he looks *into the eyes of another* or *with the eyes of another.*"[58]

Contrast this with the idea put forward by Rene Descartes in 1637, "I *think,* therefore *I am,*" which conjures up a picture of a disembodied mind, separate and sovereign over the body and the emotions. Cartesian thought had enormous influence on Enlightenment conceptions of human nature and has continued to influence Western thought up to the present day. Research by scientists in many fields in the last quarter century or so is strongly challenging this view and providing evidence to support Bakhtin's insights.

For example, Antonio Damasio has demonstrated that emotions and their biological underpinnings play a critical role in high level cognition. His findings show there is no single place within a human organism solely responsible for creating a "thought." We interact with our environment as a whole through a complex orchestration of biochemical and neural regulatory circuits operating in concert.[59] As Rifkin says, "the act of thinking combines sensations, feelings, emotions, and abstract reasoning in an embodied way. ... 'I *participate*, therefore I *am*...'"[60] is a much more accurate reflection of the reality of human experience than the Cartesian view. We engage with our entire being the people and the world around us, and out of this participation comes our thoughts, feelings, actions and our sense of self.

From the perspective of deep ecology, it is no surprise to discover that human development depends on relationship. Deep ecology holds that everything in nature exists in relation to everything else. Everything is connected and it is the relationships among the parts rather than the parts themselves that create and sustain the whole. As Rifkin suggests, systems-thinking questions the notion of free-market capitalist economics that humans act as autonomous beings, functioning independently in self-optimizing ways, each maximizing his or her own individual utility.[61] The science of ecology is challenging the Darwinian emphasis on the competitive struggle between individual creatures for scarce resources. As Rifkin notes, from an ecological perspective nature consists of symbiotic and synergistic relationships where the fate of each part is determined as much by reciprocal engagement as by any competitive advantage.

The Centrality of Emotions

In his book, *Born to Be Good: The Science of a Meaningful Life,* Dacher Keltner notes that emotions have long been a battleground for competing ideas about human nature.[62] In much of western thought emotions have been viewed as enemies that should be tamed and even banished from social life. For example, Keltner quotes B.F. Skinner: "We all know that emotions are useless and bad for our peace of mind."[63] Many of the metaphors we use to describe our emotions suggest they are adversaries not allies, causes of illness rather than health, forms of insanity not moments of understanding.

"We wrestle with, become ill from, and are driven mad by love, sadness, anger, guilt, shame, ...We assume that emotions are lower, less sophisticated, more primitive ways of perceiving the world, especially when juxtaposed with loftier forms of reason."[64]

For most of the 20th century the field of psychology focused on what are known as negative emotions like anger, anxiety, contempt, fear, shame, grief, rage, sadness, etc. Researchers and clinicians alike sought to understand the genesis and expression of such emotions largely in order to contain or minimize their negative effects on the lives of people who were "wrestling" with them. Little attention was given to understanding the role of positive emotions like empathy, compassion, love, joy, gratitude, embarrassment, awe, and happiness in human experience despite the fact that Darwin, himself, laid the groundwork for such study. In his 1872 book, *Expression of the Emotions in Man and Animals,* Darwin described in detail the expressive behaviors observed in humans in the presence of both positive and negative emotions.[65] He also observed similarities between these behavioral expressions in humans and in other animals including our primate cousins. However, he lacked data that would address whether or not facial expressions are universal within a human species shaped by evolutionary pressures.

One-hundred years later, Paul Ekman began research that would yield the data Darwin lacked, work which has led to an evolutionary approach to understanding human emotion. From this perspective emotions are understood as embodied in distinct, genetically encoded physiological processes universal to humans and shaped by our evolutionary past. Ekman and his colleague Wallace Friesen, developed the Facial Action Coding System (FACS), an anatomically based method for identifying every visible facial muscle movement in a frame by frame analysis of facial expression as it occurs in the flow of social interaction. This tool gave psychological science the first objective measure of specific emotion that could be used by labs around the world that were equipped to videotape emotional behavior and employed researchers trained in the system who could take the hour it required to code a single minute of behavior.[66] Over the course of the past 30 years, hundreds of studies on the correspondence between facial expressions and emotional states have led to a more precise understanding of the place of emotion in the brain, the role of emotion in social life, parallels between human and nonhuman emotion, and how we all have different emotional styles.

Keltner sums up the contribution of Ekman's work:

"...his papers set in motion a scientific revolution that required a radical revision of time-honored assumptions about human nature. This science began to uncover how emotions are wired into our facial anatomy, our vocalizations, our autonomic responses, and our brains. We learned that emotions support the commitments that make up the social contract with friends, romantic partners, siblings, and offspring. Emotions are not to be mastered by orderly reason; they are rational, principled judgments in their own right. Emotions do not subvert ethical living; they are guides to moral action, and they tell us what matters. Emotions like compassion, embarrassment, gratitude, and awe are the substance of ... the meaningful life."[67]

Expanding our View of Human Nature

The findings described above provide only a glimpse into a rapidly growing body of research in many fields that together give us a much fuller and more positive picture of human nature than the one that has dominated Western thinking for the past 200 years. This new understanding doesn't deny our darker instincts, but does offer convincing evidence that we are wired for compassion, kindness, fairness, cooperation, and concern for the greater good. While researchers in diverse fields continue to investigate our positive emotions, expand our understanding of the evolutionary roots of human morality and of the importance of the social aspects of our nature, they are also studying the conditions that enable these qualities to develop and flourish. The good news is that we humans already have within us the potential to live in right relationship with others and with Earth. We need to replace the social and economic institutions that now ignore, discourage, or constrain our potential for right relationship with new institutions that allow our potential for right relationship to thrive.

The scientific findings revolutionizing our understanding of human nature confirm insights about human nature that have been central to religious teachings down through the ages. Karen Armstrong writes that what unites the ethics of the world's religions is the teaching of compassion, as exemplified in Christianity by the Golden Rule.[68] The Dalai Lama has taught, "If you want to be happy, practice compassion; if you want others to be happy, practice compassion."[69] Practicing compassion is, perhaps, the fundamental expression of right relationship and a guiding principle for humans in our search for a new way to live on Earth.

Chapter 9
How on Earth Do We Live Now?

We are now experiencing a moment of significance far beyond what any of us can imagine. What can be said is that the foundations of a new historical period, the Ecozoic Era, have been established in every realm of human affairs. The mythic vision has been set in place. The distorted dream of an industrial technological paradise is being replaced by the more viable dream of a mutually enhancing human presence within an ever-renewing organic-based Earth community. The dream drives the action. In the larger cultural context the dream becomes the myth that both guides and drives the action.

—Thomas Berry (1999)[70]

How on Earth Do We Live Now? We originally posed this question as a cry of lamentation. But it is also a call to intellectual, spiritual, social, and physical action: "How on Earth do we live now? This question can be a rallying cry for all folks who are determined to steer a new course to ecological sound re-inhabitation of the planet, starting with our local and regional environments.

A new kind of "progress" is in prospect; progress in the cultivation of respect for the whole commonwealth of life, progress in the practice of nurture for that which supports life, and progress in stewardship of the gifts of Creation as we tend them into natural capital. The new progress will have an antenna for changes that enhance the common good. It will recover the archives of cultural wisdom, and develop an inventory of ecologically sound adaptation skills. Thus can the natural capital approach and the deep ecology approach together move the human enterprise into a mutually beneficial relationship with the great Creation that surrounds us.

Science and spirituality team up in deep ecology in a way that lifts up the ethic of right relationship.[71] Right relationship and resource allocation team up in natural capital in a way that lifts up respect and well-being for the whole commonwealth of life. If we can team up these understandings of deep ecology and natural capital, and keep our focus on the common good, we will have a strategy and action plan to deal with whatever is to come in the best way we can.

Quaker Contribution

True religion does not draw men out of the world but enables them to live better in it and excites their endeavors to mend it.

—William Penn (1682)[72]

William Penn is one of the figures who exemplifies the Enlightenment tradition in Christian religious thinking. Along with other early members of the Religious Society of Friends (Quakers), he transcended the conventional theological dualism of sacred and secular, and helped bring a universalist ethic of human betterment into the forefront of religious consciousness. Quakerism was a 17th Century religious innovation within Christendom, and those attracted to its new approach to spiritual life were well disposed to radical, progressive change in social and economic relations as well. Quakerism, essentially, moved spiritual life from the forms of a set theological dogma to the experience of an open horizon of learning. The Quaker innovation was not so much a new theology as a new approach to all of life—an approach that put "continuing revelation" at the center of its practice. This heritage is the context in which the authors of this pamphlet have come together around the question, "how on Earth do we live now?" This last section of our pamphlet will speak briefly to the potential of the Quaker contribution toward Earth restored, but in a way that we hope will resonate with all like-minded folks.

As the Industrial Revolution and its commercial development got underway, an emphasis on leading a practical intentional life led many Quakers to be leaders in manufacturing, the retail trades, banking and finance.[73] In farming Quakers tended to be commercial farmers with a strong interest in new horticultural techniques, better seeds and improved animal stock.[74] While these vocations and progressive practices often led to better lives for many people, it has now become clear that the "improvements" of the industrial-commercial system, were often purchased at a high price to Earth's ecosystems.

An Emerging Discipline

There is a spiritual tension between the old faith in technological progress and the growing sensitivity to the integrity of Creation. This tension is troubling not only to many Quakers, but to a wide community of people who are seeking a better way to be in relationship with the whole Earth and its commonwealth of life. We seek the guidance of continuing revelation, of ever new horizons of learning, as we cope with the practical changes that have begun to face us in day-to-day life. From an unconscious faith in technological progress we are moving to the conscious discipline of ecologically sound adaptation.

For Quakers, as for others who take up this discipline, there is much to appreciate about the concept of the commons, and the cooperative governance of the commons, because it places responsibility and accountability for equitable access to common resources on those who use them in a given locale. The governance of the commons takes into account local conditions in setting rules for use and for preserving the vitality and resilience of resources under its care. "Under the care of the commons" is a phrase that, for Quakers, may evoke another phrase, "under the care of the Meeting." There is a deep resonance of solidarity and mutual care for the gifts of Creation in this discipline.

There is a remarkable similarity between the values and practices that enabled Quakers to establish and maintain the Religious Society of Friends and the participatory, egalitarian, self-governing practices required for successfully governing the commons. Quakers were associated with Robert Owen in the founding of the Cooperative Movement in the early 19th Century.[75] Quakers have been active in cooperative ventures and enterprises ever since. Quaker experience in building trust within community settings and creating effective practices for conflict resolution are directly relevant to successfully governing the commons. By virtue of their faith community experience, Quakers should be particularly drawn to support and participate in the public trust institutions that are needed for governing the commons.

In the past, Quakers have been primarily concerned with the well-being and development of human communities, but many are now waking up to an imperative to extend our concern and caring to the whole community of life. This is reflected in efforts to re-interpret existing Quaker testimonies in the light of an ecological world-view[76] or to incorporate these ideas into a wholly new Quaker testimony on Earthcare.[77] These initiatives amplify the relevance of Quaker experience in helping to shape a realm of the commons that is responsible for overseeing the care and use of Earth's life-sustaining gifts.

In the same way that members of the Religious Society of Friends led in past social reform movements, it is time for Quakers to help lead the way in building an ecologically sound economy. In a time when prices varied widely depending upon who the buyer was, early Quaker merchants established one fair price that was available to everyone who came to the marketplace. So now, for example, as our society is engaged in a great struggle on how to drive down carbon emissions, Quakers could call on the same sense of fairness and respect with regard to pricing greenhouse gases as they are emitted into the commons of the atmosphere.

The lack of an apparent price for using the open air as a waste disposal site has led to abusing and despoiling the atmosphere. But there is a price, and it must now be made explicit and paid by all who use the atmosphere in this way, and all who benefit from such use. What price would be fair and consistent with respect for all people and the whole commonwealth of life?

Many Quakers, and many others, envision a time when the spiritual and material aspects of the human-Earth relationship co-exist in harmony and each have an important role to play in maintaining a resilient and flourishing commonwealth of life, a time when natural capital and deep ecology are both lifted into right relationship according to the common good.

Building Earth restored in an industrial economy is not an easy task. It asks several things of Friends. First of all, we must live our lives in a manner that sets an example. While this can be done household by household, collective action in creating ecologically sound communities that are also viable for the larger society remains a great challenge.

Secondly, the practice of collaborative discernment and decision making that Quakers cultivate should be brought into the public policy arena at every opportunity. Quakers hold to the experience of the Inner Light not only as a spiritual reality, but as a way of informing decision-making process. Decision making that arrives at unity, rather than majority rule, has been long practiced by the Society of Friends, and is precisely what is needed for successful governance of the commons.

And finally, in line with the Quaker insight that the Inner Light creates the potential for everyone to manifest the Spirit of God in the world, Friends firmly hold to expectation that people have the potential to choose the common good. But do we proceed with this in mind when we deal with economics and the ecology of the planet? Winning arguments about correctness should be less important than finding the common vision for action that will advance Earth restored. It is this faith in the future, this willingness to continue laboring at the task, and this belief in the inherent goodness of Creation, which leads Quakers to engage the world for radical change, knowing that the outcomes we seek will not come easily, as soon as we might like, or in exactly the way we might envision.

In 1964, Kenneth Boulding, Quaker economist and pioneer of ecological thinking, urged the Society of Friends to work at the "translation of its religious and ethical experiences and insights into a conscious understanding of the way in which the kind of love which we treasure ... can be produced, defended, and extended."[78]

This is the spiritual movement, as it were, within the social-political movement of which we are a part. Little of lasting value will be accomplished, either in economics or in ecology, that is not motivated by the kind of love and respect that makes human betterment and ecological integrity part of the same work plan. Such is the mission we have attempted here in the hope that engagement with natural capital, deep ecology, and the commons will help open a path to the future in which we can all gain a better footing.

Framing Principles for Engagement with the Commons

In our discernment we have been drawn to an understanding of how the natural capital approach to the economy, and the deep ecology approach to the human-Earth relationship, can be integrated into the reality of the commons. In order to map out what this means in a succinct way, we have developed a set of framing principles. "Framing" brings certain factors, concepts, and values into focus, which is important in our culture of information overload. Framing enables people to establish key images of understanding that, in turn, motivate behavior. The fields of study and the ranges of concern we have taken up in this project are diverse and complex.

The framing principles offered here are stated as governing principles for a mutually enhancing human-Earth relationship and for the development of human communities devoted to equity and the common good. They have helped us bring the threads of our study into a focus of ecological and ethical consciousness that can be carried forward into further learning, public dialogue, and civic action. We hope they will engage others in a similar way.

1) Earth functions as a singular, integral commons that creates, endows, and maintains all life.

2) All species have an intrinsic relationship with every other species and with the commons for access to the means of life.

3) The human species is one form of life among many with no special right to common resources.

4) All human communities have equitable access to the means of life from the common resources of the ecosystems and geographic zones in which they exist.

5) No human community, national state, or corporate entity has a right to rob, deplete or destroy the common resources.

6) National economies and the whole global economy are subsets of Earth's biospheric economy–the global commons.

7) Engagement with the commons is based on the best scientific and indigenous knowledge and guided by the precautionary principle.

8) Decision-making processes and systems of governance for managing the commons are inclusive, fair, equitable, grassroots driven, and consensus based.

9) Economic activity that engages the commons includes full-cost accounting in both monetary value and ecological integrity for all operations and transactions.

10) The commons supports the flourishing of all human and other communities of life on Earth, current and future.

Contributors

David Ciscel is a member of Memphis Friends Meeting, a Quaker Earthcare Witness Steering Committee member from Southern Appalacian Yearly Meeting and Association, and professor emeritus of economics from the University of Memphis.

Barbara Day is a member of Upper Fox Valley Friends Meeting, McHenry County, Illinois, Illinois Yearly Meeting, a member of the *Quaker Eco-Bulletin* editorial team, a retired editor on several trade press publications and owner of <oldstufftonewstuff.com>.

Keith Helmuth is a community economic development activist now retired from farming, bookstore management and college teaching. He is a founding member of the Board of Trustees of Quaker Institute for the Future, Coordinator of *Quaker Eco-Bulletin,* and a member of New Brunswick Monthly Meeting, Canadian Yearly Meeting.

Sandra Lewis is a clinical psychologist and founding member of the Ecoberries Affinity Group in Strawberry Creek Friends Meeting in Berkeley, CA, Pacific Yearly Meeting. She has been a member of the *Quaker Eco-Bulletin* editorial team since its beginning in 2001.

Judy Lumb is a retired professor of immunology and current Editor of *Producciones de la Hamaca.* She is on the editorial teams of *Quaker Eco-Bulletin* and *What Canst Thou Say.* She is still a member of Atlanta Friends Meeting, Southern Appalacian Yearly Meeting and Association, but has lived in Belize since 1987.

Endnotes *(full citations in Bibliography)*

1) Ciscel (2007)

2) Ciscel (2009)

3) This expression is associated with the vision statement of Friends Committee on National Legislation and has come to be used among Quakers to indicate a condition in which human economic activity has ceased degrading Earth's life support capacity and has figured out how to function in a way that supports and enhances the biotic integrity of Earth's ecosystems.

4) Attributed to Johann Wolfgang von Goethe (1832) <vhemt.org/ecology.htm>

5) Reynolds (1948) p. 85

6) Hau de no sau nee (1977)

7) Helmuth (1997a and 1997b)

8) Diamond (2005)

9) Chew (2001), Constanza (2007), Novacek (2007)

10) Hawken, et al. (1999)

11) Hau de no sau nee (1977) p. 3

12) Beaton and Maser (1999), Cunningham (2002), Devall and Sessions (2001), Dresner (2002), Edwards (2005), Lambin (2007), Macy (1998), McDonough and Braungart (2002), Naess (1989, 1993, 2010), Princen (2010), Robert (2002), and van Hoogstraten (2001)

13) <calacademy.org>

14) Daly and Farley (2004)

15) Daly (1991)

16) Helmuth (2009)

17) Brown and Garver (2009)

18) This metaphor is taken from the book by James Gustave Speth (2008), The Bridge at the Edge of the World.

19) Ostrom (1990)

20) Locke (1952) p. 20

21) Weisman (2007)

22) Filmer (1680)

23) Locke (1680-1690)

24) Weaver (2003)

25) Freyfogle (2007) p. 147

26) Freyfogle (2007) p. 138, 139

27) This comment by Ismail Serageldin, then Vice President of the World Bank, in a *Newsweek* August 1995 interview was picked up by other media. He intended it to raise an alarm about the impending global water crisis.

28) Gleick (2009)

29) Pearce (2006)

30) This quotation is attributed to Chief Seattle from a speech he reportedly gave in 1854. It was written from his notes by Dr. Henry Smith and published in the Seattle Sunday Star on Oct. 29, 1887.

31) Getches (1997)

32) UNESCO <unesco.org/water/news/transboundary_aquifers.shtml>

33) Barlow (2007)

34) United Nations <un.org/News/Press/docs/2010/ga10967.doc.htm>

35) Hardin (1968)

36) Ostrom (1965)

37) Ostrom (2009)

38) Ostrom (1990)

39) Dietz, Ostrom, and Stern (2003)

40) Ostrom (1965)

41) Brondizio, Ostrom and Young (2009)

42) Barnes (2001)

43) Barnes (2006)

44) Franke (1988), McKibben (1995)

45) MacLeod (1997), Whyte (1988)

46) Keltner (2009)

47) Rifkin (2009)

48) Keltner, Marsh, and Smith (2010) p.15

49) Hrdy (2009) p. 21

50) Hrdy (2009) pp. 178-9

51) Hrdy (2009) p. 28

52) Rifkin (2009) p. 142

53) Rifkin (2009) p. 83

54) Rifkin (2009) p.143

55) Taylor (2002) p. 38-9

56) Taylor (2002) p.39

57) Taylor (2002)

58) Rifkin (2009) p. 147

59) Damasio (2000)

60) Rifkin (2009) p. 147

61) Rifkin (2009) p. 596

62) Keltner (2009) p.50

63) Keltner (2009) p.50

64) Keltner (2009) p.17

65) Darwin (1872)

66) Ekman (2007) p.32-34

67) Keltner (2009) p.51

68) Armstrong (2007) Chapter 7

69) Dali Lama (2001)

70) Berry (1999)

71) Brown and Garver (2009)

72) Penn (1682)

73) Raistrick (1950), Tolles (1948)

74) Fischer (1989)

75) Morton (1969)

76) Helmuth, Lumb, Lewis, and Day (2006), and Helmuth (2008)

77) Tannenbaum, Lewis and Barnhart (2010)

78) Boulding (1964) p. 26

Bibliography

Alperovitz, Gar and Lew Daly, 2008. *Unjust Deserts: How the Rich are Taking Our Common Inheritance and Why We Should Take It Back.* New York: The New Press.

Armstrong, Karen, 2007. *The Great Transformation.* New York: Knopf Doubleday Publishing Group.

Barlow, Maude, 2007. *Blue Covenant: The Global Water Crisis and the Coming Battle for the Right to Water.* New York: The New Press.

Barnes, Peter, 2001. *Who Owns the Sky? Our Common Assets and the Future of Capitalism.* Washington DC: Island Press.

Barnes, Peter, 2006. *Capitalism 3.0: A Guide to Reclaiming the Commons.* San Francisco, Berrett-Koehler.

Beaton, Russ, and Chris Maser, 1999. *Reuniting Economy and Ecology in Sustainable Development.* Boca Raton FL: CRC Press.

Bauman, Zygmunt, 2008. *Does Ethics Have a Chance in a World of Consumers?* Cambridge MA: Harvard University Press.

Berry, Thomas, 1999. *The Great Work: Our Way into the Future.* New York: Bell Tower/Random House.

Berry, Thomas, 2006. *Evening Thoughts: Reflections on Earth as a Sacred Community.* San Francisco: Sierra Club Books.

Boulding, Kenneth, 1964, *The Evolutionary Potential of Quakerism.* Wallingford PA: Pendle Hill Pamphlets.

Brondizio, Eduardo S., Elinor Ostrom, and Oran T. Young, 2009. Connectivity and the Governance of Multilevel Social-Ecological systems: The Role of Social Capital. *Ann. Rev. Environ. Resources* 34: 253–78.

Brown, Lester, 2006. *Plan B 2.0: Rescuing a Planet under Stress and a Civilization in Trouble.* New York: WW Norton and Company.

Brown, Lester, 2009. *Plan B 4.0: Mobilizing to Save Civilization.* New York: W.W. Norton. <www.earth-policyinstitute.org>

Brown, Peter G. and Geoffrey Garver, 2009. *Right Relationship: Building a Whole Earth Economy.* San Francisco: Berrett-Koehler Publishers.

Brown, Peter G. and Jeremy J. Schmidt Eds., 2010. *Water Ethics: Foundational Readings for Students and Professionals.* Washington DC: Island Press.

Chew, Sing C., 2001. *World Ecological Degradation: Accumulation, Urbanization, and Deforestation 3000 B.C. – 2000 A.D.* Walnut Creek CA: AltaMira Press.

Ciscel, David, 2007. It's the Economy, Friend. *Quaker Eco-Bulletin* 7:4.

Ciscel, David, 2009. Steps on the Ladder to an Earth Restored. *Quaker Eco-Bulletin* 9:2.

Constanza, Robert, Ed., 2007. *Sustainability or Collapse? An Integrated History and Future of People on Earth.* Cambridge MA: MIT Press.

Cunningham, Storm, 2002. *The Restoration Economy.* San Francisco: Berrett-Koehler Publisher.

Dalai Lama, 2001. *Ethics for a new Millenium.* New York: Riverhead Trade (Penguin).

Daly, Herman, 1991. *Steady-State Economics.* Washington DC: Island Press.

Daly, Herman, 2009. <theoildrum.com/node/3941>.

Daly, Herman, and Joshua Farley, 2004. *Ecological Economics: Principles and Applications.* Washington DC: Island Press.

Damasio, Antonio R., 2000. *Descartes' Error: Emotion, Reason, and the Human Brain.* Minneapolis MN: Quill House Publishers.

Darwin, Charles, 2009. *The Expression of Emotion in Man and Animals (1872).* New York: Oxford University Press.

Davidson, Eric A., 2000. *You Can't Eat GNP: Economics as if Ecology Mattered.* New York: Perseus Publishing.

Devall Bill, and George Sessions, 2001. *Deep Ecology.* Layton UT: Gibbs Smith Publisher.

Diamond, Jared, 2005. *Collapse: How Societies Choose to Fail or Succeed.* New York: Viking Penguin.

Dietz, Thomas, Elinor Ostrom, and Paul C. Stern, 2003. The Struggle to Govern the Commons. *Science* 302: 1907–12.

Dreby, Ed, 2008. We Need a Ladder: Avoiding Depression While Downsizing. *Quaker Eco-Bulletin* 8:4.

Dreby, Ed, 2011. The Growth Dilemma. *Quaker Eco-Bulletin* 11.2.

Dresner, Simon, 2002. *The Principles of Sustainability.* London and Sterling VA: Earthscan.

Edwards, Andres, 2005. *The Sustainability Revolution: Portrait of a Paradigm Shift.* Gabriola Island BC: New Society Publishers.

Ekman, Paul, 2007. *Emotions Revealed.* New York: Henry Holt and Co.

Elliot, Herschel, 2005. *Ethics for a Finite World: An Essay Concerning a Sustainable Future.* Golden CO: Fulcrum Publishing.

Filmer, Robert, 1991. *Patriarcha (1680) and Other Writings.* New York: Cambridge University Press.

Fischer, David Hackett, 1989. *Albion's Seed: Four British Folkways in America.* New York, Oxford University Press.

Franke, Richard W., 1996. *Life is a Little Better: Redistribution as a Development Strategy in Nadur Village, Kerala.* New Delhi: Promilla.

Freyfogle, Eric, 2007. *On Private Property: Finding Common Ground on the Ownership of Land.* Boston: Beacon Press.

Getches, David H., 1997, *Water Law.* St. Paul, MN: West Publishing Co.

Gleick, Peter H., 2009. *The World's Water 2008-2009. The Biennial Report on Freshwater Resources.* Washington DC: Island Press.

Hardin, Garrett, 1968. The Tragedy of the Commons. *Science* 280 (5364): 682–3.

Hau de no sau nee, 1977. *A Basic Call to Consciousness: The Hau de no sau nee Address to the Western World, Geneva, Switzerland.* Rooseveltown NY: Akwesasne Notes.

Hawken, Paul, Amory Lovins and L. Hunter Lovins, 1999. *Natural Capitalism: Creating the Next Industrial Revolution.* Boston: Little, Brown and Company.

Heal, Geoffrey, 2000. *Nature and the Marketplace: Capturing the Value of Ecosystem Services.* Washington DC: Island Press.

Helmuth, Keith, 1997a. Earth Process and the Wish for Human Exemption. *EarthLight Magazine* Spring 1997.

Helmuth, Keith, 1997b. Will There be any Toads in Heaven? *EarthLight Magazine* Summer 1997.

Helmuth, Keith, 2004. *Arrowhead to Hand Axe: In Search of Ecological Guidance. Canadian Quaker* Pamphlet 60, Argenta BC: Argenta Friends Press.

Helmuth, Keith, 2008. "What is the Moral Assignment?" Re-Visioning the Quaker Peace Testimony. *Quaker Eco-Bulletin* 8:3

Helmuth, Keith, 2009. A Bridge to the Future: Awakening to the Reality of the Commons. *Quaker Eco-Bulletin* 9:3.

Helmuth, Keith, Judy Lumb, Sandra Lewis, and Barbara Day, 2006. Changing World View and Friends Testimonies. *Quaker Eco-Bulletin* 6:4.

Henriques, Adrian and Julie Richardson, Eds., 2004. *The Triple Bottom Line: Does It All Add Up?* London: Earthscan.

Hinshaw, Robert, 2006. *Living With Nature's Extremes: The Life of Gilbert Fowler White.* Boulder, Colorado: Johnson Books.

Homer-Dixon, Thomas, 2006. *The Upside of Down: Catastrophe, Creativity, and the Renewal of Civilization.* Washington: Island Press.

Hrdy, Sarah Blaffer, 2009. *Mothers and Others: The Evolutionary Origins of Mutual Understanding.* Cambridge: Belknap Press.

Hyde, Lewis, 2010. *Common As Air.* New York: Farrar, Straus and Giroux.

Kasser, Tim, 2002. *The High Price of Materialism.* Cambridge MA: MIT Press.

Keltner, Dacher, 2009. *Born to Be Good: The Science of a Meaningful Life.* New York: W.W. Norton & Co.

Keltner, Dacher, Jason Marsh, and Jeremy Adam Smith, Eds., 2010. *The Compassionate Instinct*. New York: W.W. Norton & Co.

Korten, David, 2010. *Agenda for a New Economy: From Phantom Wealth to Real Wealth*. San Francisco: Berrett-Koehler.

Lambin, Eric, 2007. *The Middle Path: Avoiding Environmental Catastrophe*. Chicago: University of Chicago Press.

Lanchester, John, 2010. *I.O.U.: Why Everyone Owes Everyone and No One Can Pay*. New York: Simon & Schuster.

Laxer, Gordon and Dennis Soron, Eds., 2006. *Not For Sale: Decommodifying Public Life*. Peterborough ON: Broadview Press.

Locke, John, 1952. *Second Treatise of Civil Government (1680-1690)*, Oscar Piest, Ed., Indianapolis IN: Bobbs-Merrill.

Lovelock, James, 2009. *The Vanishing Face of Gaia: A Final Warning*. New York: Penguin Books.

MacLeod, Greg, 1997. *From Mondragon to America: Experiments in Community Economic Development*. Sidney, NS: University College of Cape Breton Press.

Macy, Joanna, 1998, *Coming Back to Life: Practices to Reconnect our Lives, our World*. Gabriola Island BC: New Society Publishers.

Marglin, Stephen, 2008. *The Dismal Science: How Thinking Like an Economist Undermines Community*. Cambridge MA: Harvard University Press.

McDonough, William and Michael Braungart, 2002. *Cradle to Cradle: Remaking the Way We Make Things*. New York: North Point Press.

McKibben, Bill, 1995. *"Kerala" in Hope, Human and Wild: True Stories of Living Lightly on the Earth*. Boston: Little, Brown and Company.

McKibben, Bill, 2007. *Deep Economy: The Wealth of Communities and the Durable Future*. NewYork: Times Books, Henry Holt and Company.

Morton, A.L., 1969. *The Life and Ideas of Robert Owen*. New York: International Publishers.

Naess, Arne, 1989, 1993. *Ecology, Community, and Life Style: Outline of an Ecosophy.* New York: Cambridge University Press.

Naess, Arne, 2010. *The Ecology of Wisdom: Writings of Arne Naess.* Berkeley CA: Counterpoint Press.

Nonini, Donald M., Editor, 2007. *The Global Idea of the Commons.* New York: Berghahn Books.

North, Douglas, 1990. *Institutions, Institutional Change and Economic Performance.* New York: Cambridge University Press.

North, Douglas, 2005. *Understanding the Process of Economic Change.* Princeton NJ: Princeton University Press.

Novacek, Michael, 2007. *Terra: Our 100-Million-Year-Old Ecosystem – and the Threats That Now Put It at Risk.* New York: Farrar, Straus and Giroux.

Ostrom, E., 1965. *Public Enterpreneurship: A Case Study in Ground Water Management.* Ph.D. Dissertation, University of California at Los Angeles.

Ostrom, E. 1990. *Governing the Commons: The Evolution of Institutions for Collective Action.* New York NY: Cambridge University Press.

Ostrom, Elinor, 2009. Nobel Prize Lecture. <nobelprize.org/mediaplayer/index.php?id=1223>

Outwater, Alice, 1996. *Water: A Natural History.* New York: Basic Books.

Patel, Raj, 2007. *Stuffed and Staved: Markets, Power and the Hidden Battle for the World's Food System.* New York: HarperCollins.

Patel, Raj, 2009. *The Value of Nothing: How to Reshape Market Society and Redefine Democracy.* New York: Picador Books.

Pearce, Fred, 2006. *When the Rivers Run Dry: Water—The Defining Crisis of the Twenty-first Century.* Boston: Beacon Press.

Penn, William, 1682. *No Cross, No Crown: A Discourse showing the Nature and Discipline of the Holy Cross of Christ, and that, the Denial of Self, and Daily Bearing of Christ's Cross,* is the alone *Way to the Rest and Kingdom of God.* Ron Selleck, Ed., (2007) Richmond IN: Friends United Press.

Princen, Thomas, 2010. *Treading Softly: Paths to Ecological Order.* Cambridge MA: MIT Press.

Raistrick, Arthur, 1950. *Quakers in Science and Industry.* New York: Philosophical Library.

Reynolds, Reginald, 1948. *The Wisdom of John Woolman.* London: George Allen & Unwin Ltd.

Rifkin, Jeremy, 2009. *The Empathic Civilization: The Race to Global Consciousness in a World in Crisis.* New York: Jeremy P. Tarcher/Penguin Books.

Robert, Karl-Henrik, 2002. *The Natural Step Story: Seeding a Quiet Revolution.* Gabriola Island. New Society Publishers.

Sagoff, Mark, 2004. *Price, Principle, and the Environment.* New York: Cambridge University Press.

Seed, John, Joanna Macy, Pat Fleming, and Arne Naess, 1988. *Thinking Like a Mountain: Towards a Council of All Beings.* Gabriola Island, BC: New Society Publishers.

Sessions, George, Ed., 1995. *Deep Ecology for the 21st Century: Readings on the Philosophy and Practice of the New Environmentalism.* Boston: Shambala Publications.

Shiva, Vandana, 2002. *Water Wars: Privatization, Pollution, and Profit.* Cambridge MA: South End Press.

Simms, Andrew, 2005. *Ecological Debt: The Health of the Planet and the Wealth of Nations.* London and Ann Arbor MI: Pluto Press.

Singer, Joseph William, 2000. *The Edges of the Field: Lessons on the Obligations of Ownership.* Boston: Beacon Press.

Skeel, David, 2005. *Icarus in the Boardroom: The Fundamental Flaws in Corporate America and Where They Came From.* Oxford and New York: Oxford University Press.

Speth, James Gustave, 2008. *The Bridge at the Edge of the World: Capitalism, the Environment, and Crossing from Crisis to Sustainability.* New Haven: Yale University Press.

Sumner, Jennifer, 2005. *Sustainability and the Civil Commons: Rural Communities in the Age of Globalization.* Toronto: University of Toronto Press.

Suzuki, David, 2002. *The Sacred Balance: Rediscovering Our Place in Nature.* Vancouver: Greystone Books.

Tanenbaum, Shelley Sandra Lewis, Kathy Barnhart. An Earthcare Testimony for Friends. *Western Friend*, December, 2010, pp. 4-6.

Tawney, R. H., 1920, 1948. *The Acquisitive Society.* New York: Harcourt, Brace & World.

Taylor, Shelley E., 2002. *The Tending Instinct: Women, Men and the Biology of Our Relationships.* Times Books: Henry Holt & Co.

Tolles, Frederick B., 1948. *Meeting House and Counting House: The Quaker Merchants of Colonial Philadelphia.* New York: W.W. Norton & Co.

van Hoogstraten, Hans Dirk, 2001. *Deep Economy: Caring for Ecology, Humanity, and Religion.* Cambridge UK: James Clarke & Co.

Weaver, John C., 2003. *The Great Land Rush and the Making of the Modern World, 1650 – 1900.* Montreal: McGill-Queen's University Press.

Weisman, Alan, 2007. *The World Without Us.* New York: St. Martin's Press.

Wessels, Tom, 2006. *The Myth of Progress: Toward a Sustainable Future.* Burlington VT and Hanover NH: University of Vermont Press and University Press of New England.

Whyte, William, 1988. *Making Mondragon: The Growth and Dynamics of the Worker Cooperative Complex.* Ithaca, NY: Cornell University Press.

Wilkinson, Richard and Kate Pickett, 2009. *The Spirit Level: Why Equality is Better for Everyone.* New York: Penguin.

Quaker Institute for the Future

The Quaker Institute for the Future (QIF) seeks to generate systematic insight, knowledge, and wisdom that can inform public policy and enable us to treat all humans, all communities of life, and the whole Earth as manifestations of the Divine. QIF creates the opportunity for Quaker scholars and practioners to apply the social and ecological intelligence of their disciplines within the context of Friends' testimonies and the Quaker traditions of truth seeking and public service.

The focus of the Institute's concerns include:

- Economic behavior that increasingly undermines the ecological processes on which life depends.

- The development of technologies and capabilities that hold us responsible for the future of humanity and the Earth.

- Structural violence and lethal conflict arising from the pressures of change, increasing inequity, concentrations of power and wealth, declining natural capital, and increasing militarism.

- The increasing separation of people into areas of poverty and wealth, and into social domains of aggrandizement and deprivation.

- The philosophy of individualism and its socially corrosive promotion as the principal means for the achievement of the common good.

- The complexity of global interdependence and its demands on governance systems and citizen's responsibilities.

- The convergence of ecological and economic breakdown into societal disintegration.

Quaker Institute for the Future